"The book's very inspiring and gives you energy and wings. It's very easy to read. I recommend this book!"
— LEO VAN DER HEIJDEN —
CEO, CALVI

"The questions come from practice, the dialogues from the workplace and the answers directly help the manager. For everyone who wants to make Scrum successful!"
— PROF. DR. ARIE VAN DEURSEN —
PROFESSOR IN SOFTWARE ENGINEERING, TU-DELFT

"All you need to correctly introduce Scrum is: this book and a fair amount of guts."
— SVENJA DE VOS —
CIO, TELE2 NETHERLANDS

"This book gave me a total overview of the reasons why Scrum is successful to us. Managers, read it!"
— ERIK VAN DER MEIJDEN —
CEO, EXACT

SCRUM
—for—
Managers

RINI VAN SOLINGEN
ROB VAN LANEN

HMEXPRESS

© Rini van Solingen & Rob van Lanen, 2015
All rights reserved.

Publisher: Happy Melly Express, www.hmexpress.happymelly.com

Design by Muuks Creative, www.muuks.com

TABLE OF CONTENTS

PREFACE 9

WHY SHOULD YOU BE INTERESTED IN SCRUM? 21
    When is Scrum for you? 24
    When should you avoid Scrum? 25
    The nine most important benefits of Scrum 26
    Is Scrum a hype? 27
    Examples of the wide applicability of Scrum 28

SCRUM: HOW DOES IT WORK? 35
    Scrum and stable teams to which the work flows 38
    Scrum in twelve steps 39
    Does Scrum always work? 44
    Why can Scrum handle dynamics and complexity? 45
    Where does Scrum come from? 46

WHAT'S THE DIFFERENCE BETWEEN AGILE AND
SCRUM? 51
    What is agile? 54
    The four reasons why agile is needed 54
    Scrum brings agility by using iterations 56
    What is the Agile Manifesto and why should you know it by heart? 57
    What are the KPIs of an agile organization? 59

HOW DO YOU MANAGE SCRUM TEAMS? 65
Scrum doesn't have an official manager role 68
Primary focus on improvement 69
Aim for effectiveness, flexibility, and flow 70
The seven most important changes for managers 71

CAN EVERY ORGANIZATION ADOPT SCRUM? 77
How to apply Scrum in an existing (plan-driven) organization? 80
What about the current procedures and roles? 81
How about project budgets and year plans? 83
Flexible office spaces, part-timers, and flexible working times
versus stable teams 84
How can you adapt Scrum to your organization
(or adapt your organization to be agile)? 85

WHAT DOES SCRUM COST AND WHAT ARE THE RETURNS? 91
What is the Return on Investment of Scrum? 94
The five most important benefits of Scrum 95
The four reasons why Scrum results in a strong growth in
productivity 97
Facts don't lie 98

HOW DO YOU ADOPT SCRUM? 103
The first ten steps towards an agile organization 106
Six choices for team focus 110
When are you done with adopting Scrum? 113
What KPIs help monitor the introduction of Scrum? 114

WHAT ARE COMMON PITFALLS WITH SCRUM? 119
When does Scrum fail? 122
The ten most important pitfalls 123
Is combining Scrum and fixed-price contracts a pitfall? 125
What to do when it's impossible to subdivide the work? 126

HOW TO BUILD SCRUM TEAMS? 131
    The five things that need to be taken care of before you start a Scrum team 134
    How is the Sprint length of a team decided? 135
    Who to put in which Scrum team? 137
    Does a Scrum team really not have a project manager? 139
    How to do personnel management for Scrum teams? 140

HOW TO MONITOR SCOPE AND PROGRESS IN SCRUM? 145
    Measuring progress with results 148
    Monitoring progress and scope with a Burn-up chart 148
    Four additional devices for measuring progress 150
    What's the scope if you can constantly change it? 151
    Six measures for fixed-price Scrum 152

HOW TO BE PREDICTABLE AND PRODUCTIVE WITH SCRUM? 157
    What kind of commitments help with being more predictable? 160
    Why do we express our estimates in points instead of hours? 160
    How to realize a continuous increase in productivity? 162
    Nine measures to further improve productivity 163
    Devices to mutually compare Scrum teams 165

HOW DO YOU ENSURE QUALITY WITH SCRUM? 171
    Working in one team prevents quality issues 174
    How to decide whether the quality is good? 174
    Should you automate all quality tests? 176
    Bad quality costs time and money and causes even more bad quality 177
    What about Scrum and documentation? 178
    What about Scrum and architecture? 179

HOW DOES SCRUM SCALE? 183
    How to scale with many teams 186
    How to manage dependencies between teams 187

How to guarantee knowledge sharing between teams 188
How to do Scrum if you're not together? 189
How to do Scrum when nearly everything is outsourced? 191

HOW TO CONVINCE OTHERS OF THE VALUE OF SCRUM? 195

How to explain Scrum to customers and stakeholders? 198
Eight measures to let stakeholders experience Scrum 199
How to deal with people who refuse to participate with Scrum? 201

EPILOGUE 204

ABOUT THE AUTHORS 207

PREFACE

The first publication on Scrum appeared twenty years ago in 1995. After the first uncertain steps, the methodology has matured in the new millennium and has become a hit. More and more examples of best practices are published, the external knowledge and certification options grow, and a large number of articles and books have been published.

The authors of this book are convinced that "agility", being able to quickly respond to change, will make the difference in the coming years. Scrum is able to make a jump start with this – and we are not alone in this opinion, as you will be able to read on the following pages. Over the years, we have learned that support and vision of management is essential for becoming successfully "agile". Therefore, this book is specifically targeted at management. Indeed, managers will need to discover the importance of Scrum and what advantages they can achieve by applying it. On the following pages some of them have shared their view on it.

GUNTHER VERHEYEN AND KEN SCHWABER (CO-CREATOR OF SCRUM), SCRUM.ORG
—

Did you also hear that managers are useless or not needed in Agile? We wonder…

Indeed, the Agile movement promotes emergence. Indeed, agile software development thrives on self-organization. Indeed, Scrum has no defined role of "manager". And Scrum — after all — is the most applied process for agile software development. But is that sufficient to label managers as useless or not needed in an agile environment?

The agile movement successfully established a set of values and principles that better fit the creative and complex nature of software development. The focus is on teams, collaboration, people, and self-directed discovery. The Scrum framework provides a great foundation for organizations to grasp agility.

The adoption of agile thinking via Scrum represents a major shift in our industry. And it is still gaining traction as the context in which we have to create software becomes increasingly complex and uncertain. Even without Scrum having prescriptions for management, it is clear that the self-organizing fundaments of Scrum have a profound impact on the role, approach, and act of managing. The challenge is to discover and implement the new needs and demands for managers when the product development process is transformed to Scrum.

The book *Scrum for Managers* by Rob and Rini explains the Scrum framework to managers. It provides them with clear insights in Scrum, what it is, what it isn't. From that basic understanding, options are presented on how to deal with it as a manager. *Scrum for Managers* guides managers in discovering where their added value is when their organizations adopt Scrum for their product development and their teams grow more mature in the use of Scrum.

Perfection is an illusion. Perfection is not the goal. Gradual improvement is. This book, *Scrum for Managers*, is part of that. Read it. Learn from it. Act, learn, improve. Re-invent yourself as a manager and increase the value you bring to the organization and its teams while transforming to Scrum.

RON VAN KEMENADE
CIO, ING
—

Change happens quickly. This seems obvious, but there are clear reasons why this applies now more than ever. On the one hand, technological advances are happening faster and faster. On the other hand, customers are increasingly able to share their experiences in real-time. Examples in my sector, financial services, are the explosion of Tweets after a disruption of the payment services and the immediate feedback in the app stores when a new mobile app is released.

Companies, banks, and governments will need to finds ways to deal with this fast way to share feedback. We need to become more and more responsive. We do not have a choice.

Scrum offers an excellent way to realize this change. And not just conceptually but in the form of a real and concrete way of working. It has been my experience that the change process towards Scrum takes real effort of management and especially also a lot of personal involvement.

Scrum for Managers is a very handy book. It is written on the basis of a large number of common questions in practice. I recognize questions I have had myself and questions I frequently encounter. This book gives clear answers which have also been written in a style which is easy to read. The book is useful to anyone who needs to decide whether or not to start with Scrum. I recommend starting with the chapters which are especially about this decision (Chapters 1, 2, 5, and 8). Subsequently, you can take your time to read the other chapters.

I recommend every manager to start with Scrum. Each manager will, as I do with my teams, face unique challenges. Therefore, you should start small, learn from your initial experiences, improve your way of working, remove impediments, and most important of all, listen to the people you work with. This book helps with this.

JEROEN TAS
CEO, INFORMATICS, SOLUTIONS & SERVICES AT PHILIPS HEALTHCARE
—

Under the "Accelerate!" theme Philips is going through an in-depth transformation necessary to realize the full potential of the company. The traditional functional and product-oriented approach is gradually replaced by a customer-focused "end-to-end" approach. This requires organizational and cultural change. Multi-disciplinary teams with specialists in marketing, supply chain, IT, design, and R&D closely collaborate to realize solutions that match the specific needs of a market. Insights in market requirements need to be realized in products quickly: action!

In 2011, we decided to adapt to the new reality of agile business. Scrum was chosen for this because of its seamless connection with the needed mindsets and behaviors:

- **"Teaming up to Excel"**. Self organizing teams of seven people. These teams need to be multi-disciplinary to be able to effectively create solutions.

- **"Eager to Win"**. Every team needs to make the created value transparent and steer based on this. We prefer to measure this value in terms of the customer and market impact.

- **"Take ownership"**. Self-steering teams are the basis. The tight collaboration of disciplines increases the problem solving skills and pace tremendously.

Another important argument to choose for Scrum was the awareness that we cannot specify the needed changes in Philips in detail in advance. There is much we need to learn and discover iteratively.

Scrum's starting to quickly spread outside of the IT organization as a means to make Philips an agile company. We're convinced that making Philips agile is an important prerequisite to be able to operate successfully in the dynamic markets of today and tomorrow. For now, Scrum's the most important part of this.

Scrum for Managers is an excellent guide to learn the new way of leading which is part of the transition we are going through. The book answers the most important management questions about managing an agile organization. This book will make an important contribution to the conceptualization in the management of Philips. *Scrum for Managers* should be mandatory for anyone in a management position in a quickly changing world!

VIKRAM KAPOOR
CEO, PROWARENESS
—

At Prowareness we help our customers to be more effective with Scrum and agility among other things. We try to be in the forefront in this and we advocate the statement *"practice what you preach"* or even better *"drink your own champagne"*. We want our company to be the most agile organization in the world.

When I saw the title of this book I was a bit startled. I don't believe in the concept of managers. Managers are reactive; you "manage a situation". For me personally it is mostly about leadership. An excellent leader primarily leads himself. Leading is causing something, making something happen, and doing so in a directing fashion. To do so you need to unlearn a number of things as well and you can only do this if you stay close to yourself. Leaders need to know what stance to take in an agile environment and how best to act.

This book helps in this. It makes the challenges of a leader concrete and provides you with practical and concrete tips on how to act. In particular the dialogues, the roadmap of the transition, and the practical To Do lists at the end of every chapter have been very helpful to me.

Of course I know both authors very well and I completely support their ideas. I know how passionately they work and recognize this in this book as well. I wish you luck with the next step for yourself and your organization, as a manager or a leader. Have fun reading this book!

SIMON REINDL

PROFESSIONAL SCRUM TRAINER AND AGILE CONSULTANT

—

A recurring theme with organizations that are in the early stages of adopting an agile mindset is what do the managers do? A common misconception is that since there is no reference to managers in the *Scrum Guide*, then they must not be needed. Who will help the organization change if not the managers — but how should they do it?

This book addresses that question, in a pragmatic easy-to-read fashion. If you are looking for a helpful guide from people with practical experience, this is it. The advice in this book is based on years of experience helping organizations move to a value-driven approach — to develop the sustained competitive advantage of having an engaged motivated workforce that builds a product that delights the customer. The handy checklists at the end of each chapter provide a useful check to see if you are moving in the right direction.

WHY SHOULD YOU BE INTERESTED IN SCRUM?

SCRUM BRINGS IMMEDIATE RESULTS IN A SHORT TIME FRAME AND REQUIRES BARELY ANY PREPARATION.

― CHAPTER 1 ―

WHY SHOULD YOU BE INTERESTED IN SCRUM?

Scrum isn't magic. It's simple logic. Apply it to deliver results faster, learn how to improve these results, and last but not least, gain more satisfied customers. Achieve all this by focusing on small tasks, looking at them from the customer's viewpoint, and completing them as soon as possible.

In short, Scrum helps you deliver value to your customer quickly, bringing you many benefits and making you much more agile. But isn't this what everyone is trying to achieve? Why would the result be any different when you use Scrum? Because applying Scrum to an organization redefines the work system in an organization by introducing new roles, processes, documents, and responsibilities. These aren't added to the current system but completely replace it. The special thing about all this is that Scrum requires barely any preparation. You can start using Scrum within the existing structures right now. It's a revolutionary intervention that works, as long as you do it completely. Remember: don't put in half the effort unless you're satisfied with half the result!

In fast-changing innovative environments in which challenges are found with planning and with delivering the right quality in time and within budget, Scrum can tremendously improve things, and do it quickly.

"How can you do your work without making a plan? How can you promise to finish on a certain date without making a plan? That's impossible!"

"I don't understand what you're trying to say?"

"Well, using Scrum, right? You never know what result you'll end up with or when it's finished. How can this work for us? We have to specify a price and a completion date. It's impossible to do that without a plan!"

"I think you're mistaken! Let me try to explain. What are you going to have for lunch later?"

"Well, salad with an avocado! I made it myself this morning."

"Alright, what are you going to have for lunch on Monday eight months from now?"

"Well, I have no idea of course!"

"Exactly! But that doesn't mean you won't eat at all, right?"

"I'm not following."

"You're claiming that without a plan you won't achieve anything. But you're certain you will eat something on a date eight months from now, without knowing exactly what that will be. That's also how Scrum works. Because you're allowing yourself to make some decisions later; by enabling yourself to do so now, you can be certain it will work out."

"Come on, that's nonsense! It's completely different for us. We have to make commitments about what functionality we will deliver. We need the details to be able to do so."

"That right there is your mistake. What if I told you eight months in advance what you would eat each afternoon? That would give you absolute certainty, but it wouldn't be much fun, would it?"

"No, of course not. I want to be able to decide what I want to eat later."

"Precisely! I'll prove to you I know how to cook, and by doing so you'll trust me to postpone decisions about details. So the only thing you do need to change is your promise. Instead of promising what to deliver you'll promise that you'll solve the problem. I cannot promise you what you'll eat eight months from now, but I can promise it'll be good! That's how Scrum works. Promising to solve the problem instead of promising what exact detailed functionality you'll deliver. Of course, this does require one extra condition."

"Which one?"

"That we periodically review the taste and decide how we can improve. We do this together."

"But that isn't a problem. That's for my own benefit!"

"Exactly! Scrum defines a process in which both parties have a common goal to continuously review and improve how things are done. Do you get it now?"

"I do! Right, it's time for lunch."

"Alright, then I'll start cooking. I'll show you the end result in eight months!"

"Yeah, yeah, I know. Joker!"

When is Scrum for you?

Do you work in an environment where you're judged on results, where customers are served, or where products are being made? Do you work in an environment where products or services are often delivered late, budgets are exceeded, quality is often too low, or expectations are regularly not met? If any of these apply to you, Scrum will help you.

By introducing Scrum, you make a revolutionary intervention, solely with the aid of one result, two lists, three roles, and four meetings, which jointly make up a new framework that quickly leads to valuable results. These valuable results for your customers quickly make you more successful and make your people much happier.

In most organizations, false security is key: plans, specifications, documents, promises, etc. But this doesn't work in practice because everything changes. If it's not the requirements, it's the implementation technology. If it's not the implementation technology, it's the market. Our world is extremely dynamic and unpredictable. Still, we insist on using processes created with the implicit assumption that nothing ever changes.

In short, we use plan-driven approaches in complex, adaptive environments. One of the core properties of a complex environment is that a plan is outdated before the ink it was written with dries. And when, inevitably, something does change, we would rather stick to our outdated plans than embrace the new situation and adapt accordingly. Pretty weird, huh?

And the funny thing about all this is that the world is becoming increasingly dynamic. The market is more dynamic than it has ever been. Scrum is an excellent approach to deal with this. One of the core assumptions in Scrum is that everything changes and it defines a structured way to be flexible. In a dynamic, complex environment, Scrum is successful because the framework defines a learning component in which the framework is adapted based on empirical data. Because of this, Scrum is able to help deliver predictable and valuable results.

Scrum enables agility, to help unleash all the power in an organization.

When should you avoid Scrum?

Scrum isn't particularly useful in simple situations. When results are highly predictable and few things change (a simple environment), the added value of using Scrum is low. In such situations, it's best to just make a plan and execute it. Scrum is also better avoided when either the team or the goal are too small to make implementing Scrum worthwhile. For example, the overhead of running the framework with a team of two people is too high. However, on the other hand, Scrum concepts are always applicable based on the idea of transparency of progress, being ready to respond to unexpected events, and being able to handle uncertainty and change. If any of those are important to you, Scrum works to your advantage.

Much of our work however, involves being able to adapt to complex situations and to act in a predictable manner. Uncertainty is the factor that severely limits our ability to work predictably. When we focus our attention on a knowledge-intensive situation in general or a software-intensive situation in particular, the uncertainty is strongest with respect to implementation technology and customer requirements. The higher the uncertainty of the technology and the higher the instability of the requirements, the more chaotic the situation becomes.

A common misconception is that you shouldn't use Scrum for anything large, complex, and complicated. According to this misconception, it would be best to use Scrum for anything simple, small, and clear. In fact, the exact opposite is true. Especially in complex situations with many interdependencies, Scrum is highly valuable. This is due to the short iterations and many small steps, continually creating an integrated product. The more complex a project is, the bigger the potential impact of even a small change. If something breaks, you want to know immediately so you can take action. When in a complex environment, you simultaneously change multiple things at once, you'll have no idea what the cause is if something breaks. So Scrum is most effective for things like complex backend systems, large construction projects, and complex collaboration structures. Scrum helps to reduce complexity and emphasizes getting to working results quickly. When the situation is simple and clear, Scrum isn't really needed.

The nine most important benefits of Scrum

1. **More control of the outcome.** Using Scrum offers significant value in situations where you need to control the result. Because work is being done in short cycles or iterations – working from one stable situation to the next – the amount of control is increased. Because of this, it is possible to adjust the direction between iterations or Sprints.

2. **Opportunity to leverage new insights.** Scrum is particularly valuable in situations where you're figuring things out as you go and, as such, it would be naive to think you can plan everything in advance.

3. **Happier customers and users.** Scrum is valuable to customers and end users. They are much more content when an iterative and customer-focused approach is used. The aspects that are most important to them get priority instead of the preconceived plan.

4. **More value for less cost.** By constantly re-prioritizing all the work to be done based on value, the highest value results are reached much sooner. Moreover, often when executing a plan you'll see opportunities you didn't know existed when you originally made the plan. Consequently, you can stop when you reach an optimal return on investment (ROI) and leverage the next opportunity. By doing so, you're maximizing the amount of work you don't (yet) do, without losing any value.

5. **Shorter turnaround times.** When using Scrum, a result that solves the most important problems is ready much sooner. Consequently, Scrum offers strong benefits in delivering value soon and solving important problems quickly.

6. **Higher productivity.** Using Scrum leads to higher productivity, firstly businesswise, because more value is created for less money. Also, the team productivity increases because: focus is constantly on solving the biggest problems and improving the team itself; there are less handovers; and the team members simultaneously work on the same problem. All the waste due to things such as storing knowledge, searching for information, waiting for team members, and the "how did we do that again"-effect is cut away.

7. **Better quality.** Using Scrum requires the quality to be higher because it defines short iterations to work from one stable release to another. Therefore, errors and problems are detected and fixed much sooner.

8. **The ability to stop.** Scrum brings a lot of value in situations with large external influences and when drastic course changes are needed. Because there is a stable release at the end of every iteration, stopping is a valid option with acceptable consequences.

9. **Happier employees.** Finally, well-executed Scrum also encourages the employees to be more content. This is caused by the high degree of team self-organization but also because constantly working towards a short-term valuable end product is a great motivator.

Is Scrum a hype?

Scrum is certainly not a hype, but more of a trend. A hype is excessive attention for something with little substance. A trend, on the other hand, is a long-term development in a certain direction.

Agility is such a long-term development and Scrum is an effective approach to implementing this trend. Incorporating Scrum helps organizations take a first step towards being agile.

By saying Scrum is merely a hype, you're denying its true value. Scrum has proven its value for more than twenty years already in a wide range of organizations: from small to large, young to old, and in both the public and private sector. Examples are Microsoft, Adobe, Google, ING, Exact, Philips, and CoolBlue.

Scrum is long past being a hype. In nearly every organization you'll find people using Scrum or at least preparing to start using it. Many marketing departments, highly successful sales teams, communication departments use Scrum, and in the education industry Scrum is already getting a foothold.

Besides this, Scrum itself is maturing as well. More and more best practices are documented, books and articles are being published, and external training and certification are becoming available. The Scrum Guide itself, the original description of Scrum, is open to revisions. Jeff Sutherland and Ken Schwaber regularly publish new versions in which they incorporate experiences with Scrum in practice.

Examples of the wide applicability of Scrum

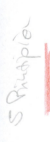

Scrum is popular, being used in a wide variety of settings, even those for which it wasn't originally intended. To make Scrum applicable in these settings, changes are made to the method and terminology but the principles remain the same: the most valuable thing first, short iterations, self-improvement, transparency, and team effort.

Scrum in education. Scrum is being deployed in secondary education using the name EduScrum. The largest adaptation is that only the teacher sets the goals and acts as a Product Owner. The students are part of self-organizing teams and are responsible for their own learning process. The results are phenomenal: motivated students, increased collaboration, and increased exam grades.

Scrum in marketing, sales, or communication. Marketing teams often work within a select number of themes and Scrum is perfectly suited for this. The teams make a weekly plan for each theme on a Scrum board in the hall. Sales teams use Scrum to process their sales pipeline and customer base. "What are we going to do this week to help all our customers advance a little bit?"

Scrum in business. Managing your entire business with Scrum? It is possible! The meetings, roles, and aids are suitable for this, as is working result-oriented with truly cross-functional teams. Marketers, salespeople, advisors, and developers can all be assigned to one team and make customers happy with valuable results using short iterations.

Scrum in public policy formulation. Making year plans can take months and many iterations. Several governments have experimented with using Scrum to do this. So they used short iterations and complete focus to make a full version of the year plan for each iteration.

Scrum for lawyers. Contracts are basically like software: they aren't physical. It's all about the collaboration. It's astonishing to see it sometimes takes companies years to finalize a contract and, in effect, also postpone the collaboration (and therefore the creation of value) for years.

Scrum in finance. It is possible to manage investments using Scrum. Don't make the entire investment in advance and wait for it to make money but rather work in short iterations. Assign a limited budget to a project for a number of Sprints and use the proceeds of the results of those Sprints to pay for the subsequent Sprints. If it's impossible to finance the subsequent Sprints by monetizing what was created in the first Sprints it might be a good idea to stop the project altogether.

Scrum to get your house ready to be sold. Crazier examples exist! One of the authors has "two left hands" and has used Scrum to get his house ready to be sold. He made a Scrum board and put everything that needed to be done in the "To Do" column. Then he invited all his friends and together they finished all the tasks via "Busy" and "Done". Fun and focused! And the last task on the list? Having a barbecue together, but... only when all the other tasks are finished!

Do you know any other examples? Let us know! It's great to see how wide Scrum is applicable and how much happiness it brings.

What should you always remember?

- Scrum is a simple intervention to work in a completely different way.
- Scrum is particularly suited for dealing with complex and dynamic situations.
- Scrum is especially suitable for large complex and dynamic systems.
- In small and simple projects that are easy to plan, Scrum is less valuable.
- With Scrum, you deliver more value in a shorter time.
- With Scrum, you face lower and predictable costs.
- With Scrum, you are able to deliver higher and more predictable quality.
- With Scrum, you can stop anytime, increasing your flexibility.
- In a fast-changing environment, you shouldn't plan details far in advance.
- Dynamics and complexity cannot be controlled by making a plan.
- By making you organization agile and flexible, you make better use of the potential of your team.
- Scrum isn't a hype but a trend.
- Scrum is widely applicable in practice.

SCRUM: HOW DOES IT WORK?

STEP-BY-STEP, WITH A STABLE TEAM, DOING THE MOST IMPORTANT THING FIRST, FINISHING EVERYTHING, AND ALWAYS BEING PREPARED FOR CHANGE BECAUSE OF IT!

— CHAPTER 2 —

SCRUM: HOW DOES IT WORK?

Scrum is simple. It consists of a single result, two lists, three roles, and four meetings in a short time frame. That's it. Scrum establishes stable teams that build towards working results in a steady rhythm (typically two weeks). To achieve those working results, we focus on completing the most important things first and showing them to stakeholders for feedback as soon as possible. By doing this, we increasingly improve our understanding of what is needed and what is the best way to accomplish it. With Scrum, we follow the rhythm of continuous improvement by getting incrementally better as a team in creating value. This is difficult and so is guiding it, hence this book.

Nothing should stop you from starting with Scrum quickly. The process of taking small steps and continuously re-evaluating what can be improved simply works. It's also scalable. This is why Scrum is a good fit for complex environments with many stakeholders, changes, unclear requirements, and/or changing technology.

There's one limitation: Every part of Scrum exists for a reason. If a single aspect of Scrum helps in your situation, it's of course good to apply it. However, that does not make what you do Scrum.

You'll only realize the full change that Scrum has to offer by implementing it completely and leaving nothing out!

"Last week I spoke to a friend of mine. He was really enthusiastic about Scrum."

"Ah well, every couple of years there's a new next best thing. First it was RAD, then RUP and now it's Scrum. I'm in the business for over 25 years now and I've seen it all come and go."

"Yeah, that was the first thought that came to mind for me as well, but there's more to it than that. There are really a lot of companies successfully applying Scrum. It started in America but now it's booming in Europe as well! I know at the bigger banks they're quite frenetic about taking up Scrum. Why do you believe it's a hype?"

"Well, frankly there's nothing new under the sun. How long have we been talking about prototyping? How many methodologies preach close customer collaboration? How long have we known it's essential to get the requirements straight as soon as possible? How long have we been talking about working iteratively? Every so often a new method comes along and this time it's going to solve all our problems for real this time. I'm not buying it!"

"Hold on a minute. All those approaches: IAD, RAD, DSDM, RUP, etcetera, where logical successors of each other. If you look at it this way, doesn't it make sense that while IT is getting even more important the need arises for something that can be applied more widely? Scrum emphasizes delivering working and tested software at least once a month. I don't see that in any of the other methods!"

"That's nonsense and you know it! Back in the day that was exactly how we used to work. We used to write software for our own department with just a couple of guys. In short cycles we used to solve our own problems and automate the work processes. That isn't new at all.

We didn't have RUPs, ISOs, SDMs, CMMIs or any of that and it worked fine!"

"Exactly! That's why I think Scrum is on to something. Back in the day, when all of that was still possible, we didn't have a thousand different roles. We didn't have business analysts who gave functional designs to information analysts. We didn't have technical designers commissioned by application architects who created a technical specification while coordinating with information managers and enterprise architects. We didn't need specifications to be validated by compliance and risk managers before the team lead could hand it over to the developers. We didn't have a dedicated test department to run regression and performance tests. And I'm simplifying things… We should return to the old ways: learning and focusing on real added value. However, we should do this in teams. The complexity of projects is orders of magnitude higher now, as is the needed technical knowledge. With Scrum we can do all this on the scale we need!"

"Yes, I believe in all that as well. But tell me: why do you think Scrum is different? Can you tell me in one sentence why Scrum isn't a hype?"

"Well, until now we used to make plans that didn't work and we ended up being late, exceeding our budget and delivering low quality. Scrum is more like we used to work before because of the tight time-boxing, continuously finishing what you're doing and working closely with customers in short cycles. It's just the scale that's bigger. Scrum really is different because, using a simple model and scalability, it leads to working results and continuously improving insights."

"That wasn't one sentence, but I'm going to forgive you for that. Let's have a more detailed look at it."

Scrum and stable teams to which the work flows

Scrum encourages cross-functional teams. These are stable teams that encompass all the necessary skills and knowledge to completely implement a certain idea in a short amount of time. What those skills and knowledge are exactly depends on the specific setting. A team with sufficient knowledge and "rowing power" (team members that really give it their all, because they are dedicated to only that team) can move mountains. This is exactly why we like to keep these teams stable, and allow the teams to improve and get well-attuned. As a result, teams become more productive.

The stockpile of work for a team is kept on a list, the Product Backlog. In each time period, which we call Sprint, a team consumes part of the work on this list. Sprints always take a static predetermined amount of time. This duration should be no longer than one month and can be chosen freely. The most common Sprint length is two weeks.

The work on the Product Backlog is never completely specified in detail. Things change, some things are still unclear, extra work can be added, or work can be discarded. The work items that are going to be worked on in the near future should be sufficiently small and clear. If not, it's difficult to work in a predictable fashion. It's sufficient for the work items for the upcoming two or three Sprints to be clear.

It's okay for the work items that are bit further out to be more coarsely defined. However, the team only consumes small manageable bites. This means that at some point the team is going to run out of work items that are small and detailed enough to work on. This could lead to the team being stuck and work to be unpredictable. Therefore, the team should constantly try to better define the future work items. The team basically works like a Pac-Man with arms, grinding the big chunks that are further out into nice little eatable dots for Pac-Man to eat when it gets to them. What's close is small, manageable, and important. What's further out may be vague and relatively unimportant for now, as long as it's small and clear when you get to it.

Working in this rhythm can be maintained indefinitely. It does require a completely different way of working. In traditional environments, we organize the people around the work. In Scrum, we do the other way around. We don't bring the people to the work but we bring the work to the people. As long as work is added to the Product Backlog, it will be consumed by the team, which can continue to work and stay intact.

Of course it's also possible to apply Scrum in projects. When doing so, do take into account it takes time to grow a performing team. If you're going to break the team up after the project, make sure this is a well-considered choice. If you do, you'll throw away the investment it took to build the team. The knowledge of the team is far higher than the sum of the knowledge of the individuals comprising the team. In the collaboration, there may exist many hidden competences. Take those into account in the decision to break the team up or allow it to continue. If the new team is only half as productive for the first four weeks, you can allow the current team to do nothing for a full two-week Sprint and still save money.

Scrum in twelve steps

Scrum defines four meetings, three roles, two lists, and one result, in one month or less.

1. **The product increment.** A working and tested result, also known as a working product. You don't necessarily have to use the result or hand it over to your customer, but if you want to, you can. This puts the focus on finishing your work! What is meant with "done" is explicitly defined in the Definition-of-Done (a checklist). Everything should always be entirely completed, leaving no loose ends. Whether the product is actually shipped is an entirely different and mostly commercial decision.

2. **The first list: the Product Backlog.** A dynamic list of all that is desired to be in the end result should be on the Product Backlog,

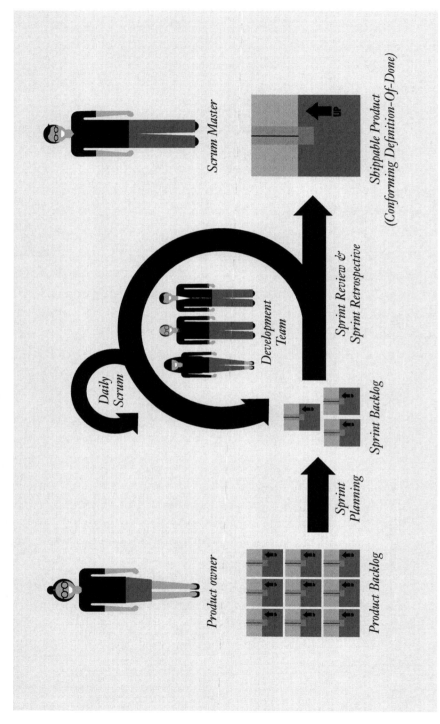

which should be explicitly ordered. The most important thing should be at the top of the list. Whatever brings the most value or eliminates the most risk is done first.

3. **The first role: the Product Owner.** Ordering the Product Backlog is difficult, especially in a complex setting with many stakeholders. Scrum tackles this by placing responsibility for this on one person: the Product Owner. By doing so, it's clear who chooses and decides. Product Owners should constantly manage stakeholders' expectations. Being able to say "No" is an important skill for a Product Owner to have. By managing expectations, prioritizing and making decisions about what work to do, Product Owner help to "maximize the amount of work not done", without losing much value.

4. **The second role: the Development Team.** The Development Team transfers ideas on the Product Backlog into working and tested products that are valuable to users. Such a team is supposed to be cross-functional; meaning that the people in the team encompass all the necessary skills and knowledge to completely implement a certain idea from the Product Backlog into a working result, within a single Sprint. The size of a Development Team is three to nine people. From ten people onwards, it's more effective to split the team into two separate ones.

5. **The third role: the Scrum Master.** It's the Scrum Master's job to make sure the Scrum framework is being used correctly and the environment is working with the team rather than against it. He or she is a coach who makes sure the team continuously improves and Scrum is embedded increasingly well into the organization. It is essential for the Scrum Master to have the authority to intervene in the execution of the Scrum process. It's fine for these Interventions to be directing rather than advisory. For self-organization to evolve, a well-intended push is often helpful.

The Scrum Master is not a project leader. Project management is a shared responsibility of the entire Scrum team.

6. **The Scrum team.** The Scrum Master, Product Owner, and the Development Team together form the Scrum team. A person can fulfill both the role of Scrum Master and member of the Development Team. Similarly, a person can fulfill both the role of Product Owner and member of the Development Team, although this is much less common in practice. It is, however, not possible to be both the Scrum Master and Product Owner. This is a rule that cannot bend aimed to prevent too strong a focus on the short term.

7. **The Sprint Planning Meeting.** The Development Team itself is best suited to decide how much work it can handle. Therefore, the Development Team forecasts how much work it'll do in the next Sprint. In the first meeting, the Sprint Planning Meeting, the team agrees a goal with the Product Owner, and then makes a plan for the upcoming Sprint. This plan consists of a list of tasks for the team to execute.

8. **The second list: the Sprint Backlog.** This list of tasks to be done in the Sprint is called the Sprint Backlog and most teams hang it on the wall as a task board. Often the columns "To Do", "In Progress", and "Done" are used. With this overview, the team members keep each other up-to-date on the progress. At the same time, the team's progress is also completely clear to an outsider. This overview is often called the Scrum board or task board, but it's just another way to visualize the Sprint Backlog.

9. **The Daily Scrum Meeting.** To make sure that this Sprint Backlog stays valid and achievable, the team discusses recent developments daily. This usually involves using three questions ("What have I achieved for the team since the last Daily Scrum?",

"What will I achieve for the team until the next Daily Scrum?", and "Is there anything getting in my way?"). In maximum 15 minutes, the team checks whether everything is going smoothly and whether reaching the end result of this Sprint is still attainable in the remaining time. If not, the plan should be changed because without a working result at the end of the Sprint, there's no value. Therefore, the plan should be re-evaluated daily.

10. **The Sprint Review Meeting.** By following the framework, the Development Team creates a new working version of the end result in every Sprint. They show the result to the stakeholders and end users, because they need their feedback. This is done in a meeting: the Sprint Review. The goal of this meeting is getting feedback on the result of the past Sprint because this will help improve both the team itself and the Product Backlog. To accomplish this, the Product Backlog is explicitly discussed. It's essential that the team and the Product Owner jointly present the result to the stakeholders. It should explicitly not be a presentation by the Development Team to the Product Owner! By doing it this way, the team's importance is reaffirmed and there's a true outside-in collaboration.

11. **The Sprint Retrospective.** From each and every Sprint we can learn a lot. We need to keep learning to continuously improve what we do. Therefore, after every Sprint, the Scrum Team takes some time to review the sprint and look for things that can be done better in the next Sprint. This meeting is called the Sprint Retrospective. The result of this meeting are points of improvement that will be implemented by the Scrum Team in the next Sprint. These points of improvement are directly placed at the top of the Sprint Backlog for the next Sprint.

12. **Product Backlog Refinement.** Officially, there is no meeting for refining the Product Backlog (remember, to help create

manageable dots for the Pac-Man to consume). In practice, however, teams often do plan a meeting for this, usually about two–four hours each week. In this meeting, the Development Team, together with the Product Owner and the involved end users, chop up the coarse items on the Product Backlog into smaller, more manageable items and estimate the amount of work.

That's it! Scrum in twelve steps. Interested in reading more about the inner workings? Then read *The Power of Scrum,* an introduction to Scrum in the form of a novel by Jeff Sutherland, Rini van Solingen, and Eelco Rustenburg. You can also download the official *Scrum Guide* on Scrumguides.org. It's free!

Does Scrum always work?

No, of course not. Scrum isn't the Holy Grail, or the answer to all your problems, or that "silver bullet" you've been looking to find for years. Scrum does help in making things clear and attainable. Implementing Scrum makes a couple of things painfully clear. This transparency uncovers many dysfunctions and puts them right into the open, each and every Sprint. And this can be painful and sometimes requires a rigorous change in thinking and how work is being done. Much of what we're used to doing is based on the principles of "getting it right in the first go" and "the plan should always be followed". We have to unlearn this.

We can only do this if we:
- **Really change the rules of the game** – from only being done at the end to everything we do is finished, and from organizing people around the work to guiding the work towards the people.
- **Start working in cross-functional teams** – building high performance, self-organizing, and self-improving Scrum teams.
- **Make results directly visible and transparent** – always having working results and everything in the process transparent and clear.

- **Constantly focus on quickly delivering value for our customer** – so measuring direct business value. Try to monetize this while you're at it.
- **Start working step-by-step while trying to learn from each and every step on the way** – don't do everything at once and find out at the end whether we succeeded, but take it one step at a time and periodically check whether things are progressing as we expected. Learning by doing is what we're trying to do and that's more difficult than it sounds!

Why can Scrum handle dynamics and complexity?

Scrum is perfectly suitable for a complex and dynamic environment because Scrum helps in responding to change and creating working and valuable results on the way. By working using a sequence of iterations, it's possible to leverage what is learned in one iteration and immediately apply it in the next. By doing so, it becomes increasingly simple to create a working result. You create a certain routine in slowly chewing through a complicated problem bite by bite, while being able to respond to change while doing so. You're prepared for change and that's the strength of the empirical approach. That is the true power of Scrum.

Scrum is particularly suited for complex work because it:
- prepares you for future changes
- chops a large problem into a series of many smaller problems
- works with cross-functional teams and, as such, helps tackle complex problems by looking at them from many different angles
- is based on what will work and, as such, helps to create a working solution as soon as possible
- brings problems to the surface fast and early so that they can be dealt with
- works with static time-boxes and, as such, makes meeting deadlines much more predictable

However, all this doesn't imply that executing Scrum is easy. It also doesn't imply that everything will go smoothly. You'll find that not everyone will understand it right away and so you'll meet resistance. You'll also encounter Product Owners with too little authority and face all the consequences from this inability to make and hold a decision. You'll encounter how hard it is to keep teams stable and have problems with quality because of this. And I haven't even mentioned problems with knowledge transfer and documentation.

At the same time, there isn't much choice. In complex and dynamic environments, making a plan isn't that useful either, because the plan is constantly caught up by reality. Building knowledge and skills with Scrum does help. It will take a while before everyone truly gets it. But is that a reason not to do it?

Where does Scrum come from?

Jeff Sutherland came up with Scrum when he was a director with Easel Corporation. Together with Ken Schwaber, he further operationalized and published the method. Based on the need to quickly produce results and to discover what software features performed better in the market than others did, Jeff set out to find a solution.

That solution came from an unexpected source. In the *Harvard Business Review* article by Takeuchi and Nonaka, "The New New Product Development Game" published in January 1986, Jeff discovered the way in which the most effective teams in the world worked. The paper by Takeuchi and Nonaka also contains the first mention of the term "Scrum", not as an approach but as a metaphor for a team that reaches the maximum based on the strengths of its individual members.

This metaphor is the reason for Scrum's name.

The way Jeff worked at Easel Corporation shares many characteristics with the approach used by Ken Schwaber at his company. Together, Jeff and Ken defined Scrum and they still maintain the definition of Scrum at www.scrumguides.org. Jeff Sutherland and

Ken Schwaber were also both present at the drafting of the *Agile Manifesto* in 2001.

Following the initial Scrum publication in 1995, it has taken a few years for Scrum to gain popularity. The most important cause for this is the publication of the book Ken Schwaber wrote with Mike Beedle in 2002, *Agile Software Development with Scrum*. After this publication, adoption rapidly accelerated.

Later books by Jeff and Ken that paint a good picture of Scrum are *Working Software in 30 Days* and *The Power of Scrum*. Also Mike Cohn "signature series" of books and the training and certification programs by the Scrum Alliance and Scrum.org have helped in increasing the wider application and popularity of Scrum.

What should you do?

- Explore how and why Scrum works, for example, by reading the *Scrum Guide* by Jeff Sutherland and Ken Schwaber.
- Memorize the Scrum terminology and make sure you understand how the Scrum cycle works and why Scrum is a meticulous interplay that you can't separate.
- Plan an introductory session in your organization to introduce Scrum and decide what role the agile approach can play in your organization to achieve results faster.
- Jointly decide whether the agile approach will make the difference in your organization.
- Don't adapt Scrum. First experience how and why Scrum works the way it does yourself.
- Make an implementation approach with the help of an experienced Scrum consultant or Agile coach.
- Try Scrum out in a project, preferably in your own team.
- Start by executing the first tasks on the implementation approach.
- Take into account that learning new things involves trial and error. Be prepared to fail. Be prepared to succeed.

WHAT'S THE DIFFERENCE BETWEEN AGILE AND SCRUM?

AGILE IS TO SCRUM AS SODA IS TO COCA-COLA

— CHAPTER 3 —

WHAT'S THE DIFFERENCE BETWEEN AGILE AND SCRUM?

The terms agile and Scrum are often used interchangeably. This is incorrect but also quite understandable. Agile has to do with agility, to be able to opportunistically change directions when needed, and flexibility. Agile can be compared to "fitness". Everyone's fit to a certain degree. But at the same time, everyone can always increase their fitness.

Scrum is like an exercise plan to increase your fitness level. A plan that is right for most people and is also used by most people. Is it the ultimate plan? Is it the only plan? No, of course not. However, striving for fitness is a fine plan for most people to get started on. Using Scrum helps you as an organization, department, or team apply an intervention to become more agile. By using Scrum, you're forced to get a number of things completed without being explicitly told how this should be done. It helps you to break free of the constraints and assumptions of the current situation and start to work in an iterative, value-oriented, and continuous learning fashion.

Applying Scrum doesn't guarantee you'll become agile, but it's an excellent first step.

"We have to start using Scrum in our entire company!"

"We do? Why?"

"Well, the use of Scrum at other companies has shown that it more than halves the number of failing projects, so we should train everyone to work using Scrum!"

"Wait a minute; I think you're getting ahead of yourself here."

"Why do you think that?"

"I think there's an error in your logic along the lines of: 'A cow has four legs, so we should be able to milk a table!'. You're making Scrum out to be a trick. A gimmick. You seem to believe that as long as we teach everyone this trick, things will automatically improve. But that's not the point of Scrum. It's about agility. We should do everything in our power to become more agile as an organization. That's what our customers need. Our customers don't need us to use Scrum. They need us to better listen to what they need and be able to deal with their changing requirements!"

"So you're saying I should train everyone in being agile?"

"That would be a good idea. Don't forget to include the entire senior management team and all other managers as well. That's the only way to really evolve as an organization. Scrum will help you in doing so, but Scrum is definitely not the end goal. The end goal is to increase agility."

"But how will we know when we're done? How long will this take? All I'm saying is that sending our people to a Scrum training only takes two days."

"Yeah joker. Like you really think two days of Scrum training is all it takes. That's like giving a driver's license to people that have passed the theoretical exam but have never driven a car and allowing them to teach others how to drive. I know you're not that naïve. Agility isn't something you can reach; it's a path."

"So, what are you saying I should do?"

"I would like to give an agile awareness workshop at your company. Half a day should be plenty. I would urge for the management team to participate as well. If you can't make room in your schedules we can also do it at night or on a Saturday. Having everyone there is really important."

"Okay and what will you teach us in the workshop?"

"I will guide you towards the right outcome. Together we will find out what is stopping us from reaching our goals. We will do a number of exercises that will show everyone it's the current way of working that is blocking us from becoming more agile. Finally, we will make a plan with the necessary steps we need to take to improve. So, what do you say? Want to do it?"

"Well, why not? And you know what? We already planned a meeting for the entire management team in two weeks anyway. Weren't you going to be there as well?"

"Yes, that's right."

"Well, let's just add a session to that meeting and let you do your thing. If you're able to convince more people, we will repeat the session for everyone in the company. Do we have a deal?"

"Yes!"

What is agile?

Agile is a term that means to be maneuverable, flexible, and fast. Agility has to do with being able to change course at any time. It's about being able to quickly and deliberately respond to change without any issues. Agility is the way to be successful in dynamic settings where everything is in a state of flux. It enables you to absorb the changes and turn them to your advantage.

An agile organization can be defined as an organization with the ability to be fast and flexible while focusing on content and reliable results. Such an organization is skilled in dealing with unexpected changes and events, market opportunities, and customer needs. It's built on processes and structures that anchor adaptability, predictability, and speed right at the heart of the organization. By doing so, the organization creates a strong competitive advantage for itself in dynamic and unpredictable markets.

In short, you'll never be fully agile as it's always possible to improve. Many organizations take the first steps towards agility by using Scrum. This is highly successful. So, introducing Scrum is a good mechanism to become more agile. Time will tell what successive actions should be taken, as you check your progress every Sprint.

The four reasons why agile is needed

Making a detailed plan and executing it to the letter only works in completely predictable situations. Unfortunately, this is no longer the case in most settings. In fact, nowadays there are many environments so dynamic that things never go according to plan and the optimal approach is to be agile. There are four important reasons for this:

1. **Knowledge work is too dynamic to plan in advance.** Knowledge work has to do with things such as organizational schemas, processes, contracts, collaboration agreements, business models, IT systems, and software. In short, knowledge work has to do with non-physical things. These aren't made out of steel, concrete, wood, or rock. They aren't

hard but soft. The great thing about this is that it's free to send such items across the world in less than a second (transport is free). At the same time, it's also free to duplicate such artifacts (no material costs). This is unique and rigorously different from the assumptions on which all existing management theories and models are based. These theories and models are based on the physical world and its limitations. But these limitations no longer apply! Because of this, knowledge work is much more flexible and dynamic and cannot be planned in advance. There's simply too much that happens on the way.

2. **We know too little in advance to make a good plan.** When building non-physical products, it's almost impossible to make a good plan in advance. You'll discover and learn what to do as you're doing it. At the start, your knowledge is lowest so this is the least appropriate time to make a plan.

3. **The world around us changes at a blistering pace**. The pace of change is enormous. The telephone took 75 years to reach 50 million users following its invention. Nowadays a successful application often reaches 50 million users in less than 75 days. Therefore, you need an approach in which you constantly keep planning and in which you only make plans for the short term. In that short term, you need to create a working result and, based on it, you make another short-term plan towards the next working result. In short, fast iterations with working results.

4. **Knowledge work isn't production work**. For years we've assumed that we can consider knowledge work to be production work. If this were true, using a plan-driven approach would make sense. However, knowledge work is characterized by continuous design decisions. A process in which design decisions are taken up until the very end is

very unpredictable and therefore difficult to plan. Using an empirical approach, however, makes much more sense. Just consider the following: when two independent teams receive the same request, will they come up with the same solution? No! The solutions will be different in every possible dimension. Working in short iterations is much wiser. In production work, there's a traditional division between thinking and doing. With knowledge work, this division doesn't exist. Knowledge work is simultaneously thinking and doing. And at the same time, you should also continuously learn how to think and act better in the future.

Scrum brings agility by using iterations

The underlying idea of using short iterations is to bring the team into a rhythm in which they constantly finish everything. We try to put teams into a rhythm of Sprints in which they constantly improve the value of the end result, one step at a time. This is why iterations are essential.

We sometimes explain this by looking at the difference between a submarine and a dolphin. When working using a traditional approach with a single plan-driven cycle, there will be a single result at the very end. In this approach, the team is like a submarine. Between the start of the work and the delivery date, the visibility is low. At the very end, the submarine surfaces and deploys its payload. In practice, that payload is never exactly what is needed and usually the submarine doesn't surface in time either. Before the submarine emerged from the depths we had no idea whatsoever about the current status of the work.

Therefore, we ask Scrum teams to work like a dolphin: they should continuously come to the surface for air. And every time they do, we ask them to show what they made so far. This significantly improves visibility. The iterations are called Sprints. By working in short Sprints, the progress of the work is much more visible. We measure the progress with working results.

But pay attention! It's not just about Scrum, it's about agility, maneuverability. This is only achieved if teams really finish everything they do, so not like in a traditional project, being done at the very end, but being done all the time. Every Sprint results in a (valuable) gift. After the first Sprint, this gift is only small, but every Sprint the gift increases in size and value. Working in this fashion guarantees you're able to deliver at any time, whatever happens. This completely eliminates the risk of missing a deadline. And you can also completely change course halfway through the project! At every point in time, you're free to work on something completely different. This is what defines agility. If you really finish each and every Sprint, you can decide to stop at any time and work on something else! What you have worked on before isn't a loss because it works and is a completely finished product in its own right!

Many companies are working with Lean and Flow on their entire value chain. Scrum is an implementation of this approach and helps by bringing a rhythm to the product development. The great thing about Scrum is that the short cycles result in a self-learning system that pulls the entire value chain along. Because everything is truly finished in every Sprint, you'll find that you achieve way more while doing less work. In general, it takes a while to truly get this, but that is one of the huge benefits of using Scrum.

Therefore, it's important to aim at being more agile and not just at using Scrum. Before you know it, the focus is back on meetings, roles, and lists without knowing what you're doing it all for.

What is the Agile Manifesto and why should you know it by heart?

The Agile Manifesto describes the value system underpinning agility. It consists of four values and twelve principles. The four values are:

> **INDIVIDUALS AND INTERACTIONS** *over* **PROCESSES AND TOOLS**
> **WORKING SOFTWARE** *over* **COMPREHENSIVE DOCUMENTATION**
> **CUSTOMER COLLABORATION** *over* **CONTRACT NEGOTIATION**
> **RESPONDING TO CHANGE** *over* **FOLLOWING A PLAN**

While there is value in the items on the right, we value the items on the left more. Next to these four values, the *Agile Manifesto* also consists of twelve principles. We won't reiterate those here but you can find them at *www.agilemanifesto.org*.

A nice tidbit is that the order of the principles in the *Agile Manifesto* isn't random. First, make sure you manage to place individuals and interactions over processes and tools. If you manage to do that, you should be able to collaborate in such a way to produce working software. Subsequently, things also become interesting for your customer and you should involve him in the collaboration and tune the result based on his needs. Finally, if you figured everything out, you're ready to tackle change.

Scrum isn't very extensive. It's a small set of rules, just like the game of chess only specifies a limited set of rules. When you start applying the rules in practice, however, you'll come across situations in which you won't know what to do. In such a situation, the answer can always be found in the *Agile Manifesto*.

Therefore, it's important to know the *Agile Manifesto* by heart. Print it out. Put posters on the wall. You can also point to it when someone complains to you: "This wasn't the plan!", "That wasn't in the document!", or "Our standards won't allow that!". In the end attitude is everything in agility. It's about what you do and why – it is a new mindset.

In practice, you often hear that using Scrum requires a cultural change. It's true that changing the way of thinking in an entire organization can be difficult and take some time. Making the new value system explicit helps in this process.

It's impossible to realize an agile culture without knowing the underlying value system!

What are the KPIs of an agile organization?

It's of course impossible to consistently answer this question. The KPIs (Key Performance Indicators) will be different in every organization and will need to be discovered. What is certain is that they usually aren't impact indicators. Profit, revenue, shareholder value, and stock price are not good KPIs. This is because they don't help you to decide what action to take, so you cannot use them to decide what course to take. They only show the final results of actions you've taken in the past.

Recently, Towo Toivola presented F-Secure's four KPIs for operation control:

1. **Value throughput.** The amount of value that is added and delivered for each Sprint. This is aggregated across all teams and measured in direct value to the customer. How much value are you delivering to the customer? In other words, are you helping your customer to deliver value to its customers?

2. **Customer satisfaction.** How happy do we make our customer? What percentage of our customers promotes us to other (potential) customers? The Net Promoter Score (NPS) is an indicator that is often used to express this KPI.

3. **Delivery time.** How long does it take on average before we have converted an idea into working and tested results? What's the maximum amount of time it takes us? How about the minimum?

4. **The amount of unfinished work.** How much of our work is partially completed? How much of our invested energy still exists in the form of unfinished work and therefore provides

no value to our customer? This should be minimized because it slows down the creation of value.

The aim is to maximize the first two of these KPIs, so you monitor their size and growth. The last two should be minimized so you monitor their size and decrease.

If you manage to control just these four parameters – profit, revenue, growth, and market – leadership will come naturally as well. Perhaps it's a good idea to use these four as a starting point and learn the rest as you go?

What should you do?

- Remember that using short iterations in which the work is truly finished is the way to becoming agile.
- Know the *Agile Manifesto* by heart.
- Advertise the *Agile Manifesto* in your entire organization.
- Put up posters with the *Agile Manifesto*.
- Correct incorrect behavior and explain why they are behaving "right" instead of "left" so people will start to correct each other's behavior in the same way as well.
- Organize an Agile Quiz with the help of a Scrum consultant or Agile coach.

HOW DO YOU MANAGE SCRUM TEAMS?

ALWAYS ASK TEAMS FOR WORKING RESULTS AND HELP THEM WITH CLEARING ROADBLOCKS

— CHAPTER 4 —

HOW DO YOU MANAGE SCRUM TEAMS?

In a Scrum team, everyone in the team takes on management tasks. This relieves you as a manager of these tasks. Because of this, quite a lot changes for you. However, this doesn't limit your ability to steer the team. With Scrum, you gain access to a completely new instrument: steering based on working and tested results that are truly finished.

Scrum teams deliver a working and tested result every Sprint. So they don't just deliver the end result after a year, but a small extra step every month or less. But remember, they only deliver results that are truly finished! This expands your ability to steer so greatly that using a process of control loses much of its importance. Therefore, this can, for the most part, be done by the Scrum teams themselves. At the same time, it's essential that teams continuously improve.

This is the critically important role that you as a manager play – helping the team improve by removing obstacles for them. You help create an environment that the Scrum team can work in. This means you should hold yourself back from intervening too much. Explain the set of rules they should follow and why they should follow them, and allow the team to organize itself within this set of rules.

You can steer based on the finished results and by helping the teams to improve every single Sprint.

"Hey, quick question: management has asked me to look into Scrum. They think the concepts match my department very well."

"Cool! Nice to hear management is waking up to this."

"Well, yeah on the one hand it's nice. One the other, however, I want to prevent having Scrum imposed on me. I don't believe that works. To me, Scrum is a means to an end and not an end goal."

"I couldn't agree more. Did you want me to confirm that?"

"Well, no, I'm wondering about the role of manager. I looked into Scrum and I really believe that working as a team towards short term results is a good idea. I also see how the three roles balance each other out: one Product Owner who makes the decisions, a self-organized development team collaborating to create a working and tested product, and a Scrum Master to guard the process."

"So what's your question?"

"Well, what am I supposed to be doing? If I look at the overall picture, they will all work it out amongst themselves with nothing left for me to do. At the same time, I don't believe my teams will be able to do this right from the start. On the one hand, they should figure this out for themselves but they aren't self-steering yet. On the other hand, I can't go and make the decisions for them, because doing so will prevent them from ever becoming a self-steering team. How do others manage this?"

"Ah, right I recognize that, it's the big management dilemma between intervening and allowing for self-steering. When do you intervene and how do you get your teams to take on responsibility?"

"Exactly!"

"Well, the truth is, it's not that hard. You'll get it when you see it. You simply transfer some of your tasks to the team. So you're completely sure what they'll be doing."

"Huh?"

"What you're doing right now, is deciding how to setup the process based on the set of rules imposed on you by your superiors. Well, you're going to let the team do that. It's your task to define the set of rules."

"Is that it?"

"Well, no, that's only the first step. There's two more after that. First there's getting the result they're responsible for to be visible. In the end all that counts is what results are delivered. Second, you're going to have to help them."

"Help them? With what?"

"Help them with getting better. Scrum teams will only increasingly deliver more and more value if they continuously get better in what they do. This means you should help them to get better. This can be by providing them with the means to do so, but also by eliminating problems they can't solve themselves."

"Kind of like a coach?"

"Yes, exactly like a coach! You're helping them train to get increasingly better in what they do, but in the end they're the ones that have win the big game. Learn them to steer themselves and help them get better at it. That will be your new role. Sounds good, right?"

"Actually, yes, it does! Helping my people to get better and eliminating impediments. Sounds like fun!"

Scrum doesn't have an official manager role

Scrum doesn't have an official manager role. Scrum only defines Product Owners, Scrum Masters, and Development Teams.

The Product Owner focuses on the "what" and "why", the Development team focuses on "how", and the Scrum Master makes sure everything in the process is going smoothly and continuously improves. Together they form the Scrum Team, which completely manages itself. When there are many Scrum Teams, the Product Owners of the different teams coordinate and prioritize between the teams and elect a Chief Product Owner when necessary to make final decisions in difficult cases. The Scrum Masters coordinate collaboration between the teams and sometimes elect a Super Scrum Master for supporting the learning process across team boundaries.

As always, practice is often more difficult than theory. Organizations are stuck with predetermined structures in which managers play a prominent role. Transitioning from a hierarchical organization with managers to an organization with self-steering teams isn't without obstacles and takes some time. In fact, many organizations that are very interested in Scrum don't (yet) have the ambition to become a fully agile organization. It's often unclear whether this ambition will ever arise at all. The more prominent the ambition is to become an agile organization, the higher the importance to heavily rely on Scrum teams. The specific circumstances will determine the best way to structure the organization.

The most important job of the manager in Scrum is to define the set of boundaries of the self-organizing teams. Part of this is creating a culture in which it's normal to work in teams towards results while continuously improving. By doing so, the manager is able to steer the teams towards becoming better. That's nice for the manager, because who's judged on growth again? That's right, the manager! So, allowing the manager to primarily focus on increasing the success of his or her teams is an important secondary advantage of using Scrum.

Primary focus on improvement

The purpose of the manager is to help teams to improve. However, the responsibility for producing results always lies with the Scrum team itself. This enables the manager to focus on getting better at producing results.

In the terms of the late Stephen Covey: production versus production capability. Or in regular English: chopping trees versus sharpening your axe. Everyone knows that working smarter beats working harder. Chopping harder and harder with a blunt axe is a far worse tactic than taking the time to properly sharpen your axe before you start chopping. It's very effective to take the time to structurally take away quality-related issues (technical debt).

This is the role of the new manager: constantly focusing on "sharpening the axe", focusing on production capability over production. This works because the manager knows that by improving these capabilities, the team will produce more with less energy. In the pre-Scrum situation, the manager also knew this, but was responsible for production as well. When choices need to be made between short-term urgency and long-term benefits, often the short term prevails. Scrum splits these two responsibilities: the Scrum teams focus on short-term results while the manager focuses on improving in the long term.

In this, it is important to differentiate between large roadblocks (impediments) and small ones (issues). We expect Scrum teams to deal with everyday issues themselves and improve their own environment as far as they're able to do so. This is not the manager's job. The manager's job is to resolve impediments. Examples are securing a budget for setting up a representative test-environment and setting up "customer days" in which Product Backlog workshops are given.

We expect the manager to continuously look out for things that could impede the Scrum teams, so they can resolve them. He or she should resolve at least one impediment in each Sprint. By doing so, the working environment of the Scrum teams increasingly improves, allowing them to realize more results, faster. In short, the manager no longer focuses on production but rather on production capabilities. A "sharpened axe" is the primary result of this.

Aim for effectiveness, flexibility, and flow

In traditional work approaches, work is continuously handed off from one person to another. Those who think up something hand it over to designers, who hand it over to builders, who hand it over to testers, who hand it over to senders, who finally hand it over to the customer. The big drawback of such chains is the isolation. Everyone can do valuable work in their own isolated subtask, while at the same time adding little value for the customer. You should look at an organization as a "value chain" and wonder: which of the links in the chain actually add value?

The main problem with such a chain becomes clear when you try to individually improve each of the links. Because when you try to make each of the links as efficient as possible, the entire chain ends up being slower. The cause of this is every link in the chain will start accumulating a stock of work. Doing nothing is inefficient, so a backlog of work will help in working continuously and efficiently. So, the more efficient each link in the chain becomes, the longer it takes for the entire chain to be passed through.

In the end, it's not the efficiency that decides the success of a chain, but rather the effectiveness! This is sometimes called "*concept to cash*" or the flow rate of a chain. The faster we can work out a concept into a result, the more effective and, therefore, the more agile!

Let's explain the importance of effectiveness over efficiency when considering a highway. What is the most *efficient* use of a highway? Ironically, a traffic jam! And preferably, a very long traffic jam that's barely moving. In that case, every piece of road is optimally used. It's not effective but extremely efficient. The most effective use of a highway is when the number of cars on it is such that everybody can get from A to B in as short a time as possible. So the best use is: flow!

If you focus on effectiveness, you will get efficiency for free in the places it matters. Just like in traffic. On large intersections it pays to be efficient, but only when effectiveness is maintained. Being efficient on large sections of straight highway? Please don't. I like to drive on! Good examples of free efficiency are the so-called desire paths. The roads are built to be effective and people create cut-through paths to be more efficient. People will automatically strive for efficiency and steering them to do so is therefore unnecessary.

The seven most important changes for managers
1. **Make sure your teams understand the "why"**. Help Product Owners master their vision and use it in making Backlogs, putting them on the wall (making them visible), and going through them with customers and stakeholders. Make sure everyone knows when they're successful.

2. **Make sure teams focus on working results.** Always go to the Sprint Review. And try not to go alone: regularly take your own superior with you or invite the director of a customer. Nothing is better in providing insight than actual results. Engage in the meeting and provide the Scrum team with feedback.

3. **Trust your team and help them where needed**. In the end, it's essential to make sure your teams get the confidence they need to organize themselves. They should understand that while they're responsible, making mistakes is normal and won't have personal consequences. Position yourself as support for resolving problems. You can, for example, hang an Impediment Backlog on your door with the impediments you're currently working on.

4. **Lead by example in agility.** Prioritize everything, time-box, finish everything completely, hang the Agile Manifesto in your office. Make "getting better" the primary goal, not just for your teams but for yourself as well. Take

initiative in celebrating parties: turn the spotlight on positive results and exemplary behavior. Make everything open for discussion and transparent. But above all, reward making mistakes and *learning from them*. Show that making mistakes is essential to be able to learn and grow. To be able to be credible enough to lead the agile changes, you'll need to show exemplary behavior.

5. **Make sure your teams understand they're responsible.** Don't ever make detailed decisions for them. Even when you see the team make a choice you consider wrong, allow them to make that mistake, unless it is safety critical. Ask them questions about how and why but do not intervene. Even if it works out like you thought, it's fine. You've just confirmed that they, and not you, are indeed responsible. Furthermore, allow them their own learning process. You learned by making mistakes as well.

6. **Make team accomplishments transparent.** Arrange for overviews in which teams and people can judge themselves. Make how things are going transparent – whether good or bad – and don't intervene. Again, asking questions and defining boundaries is fine. If teams aren't able to be successful within those boundaries, then adapt them. But keep the team responsible for its own work within those new boundaries. The HR-cycle could become more frequent and, next to the individual, also focus on the team.

7. **Make sure teams strengthen their capabilities and coach them in doing so.** If teams should improve, individual team members should work on their skills as well – taking courses, reading books, and experimenting. So, the teams should be provided with the time and space to do these things. You can choose to provide teams with their own training budget.

If you do this, the team members can decide together how best to employ those funds for the good of the team. Really see yourself as the coach for these teams. How can you best help them in getting the best out of themselves?

What should you do?

- Give teams the confidence and room for self-organization.
- Grant everyone the opportunity for their own learning process and don't intervene.
- Make sure all results are always transparent.
- Focus on providing value for the customer.
- Aim for effectiveness, value, flexibility, and flow.
- Provide boundaries within teams arrange their process.
- Make team improvement your goal.
- Lead by example by also using a transparent list (backlog) yourself.
- Help teams by resolving impediments.

CAN EVERY ORGANIZATION ADOPT SCRUM?

SCRUM FITS ALMOST EVERYWHERE. ACHIEVING FAST AND VALUABLE RESULTS IN A TEAM IS ALWAYS RIGHT!

— CHAPTER 5 —

CAN EVERY ORGANIZATION ADOPT SCRUM?

While Scrum is originally from the IT sector, it can be applied much wider than that – throughout the organization. Because of the success stories of software teams, people from many other disciplines start adopting Scrum as well. Often they start within their own discipline and, as a result, restrict it to optimizing one of the links in the chain, but you have to start somewhere. Some companies take it so far that they use Scrum for running their entire business: fully cross-functional teams that together service a market or a group of customers.

At a first glance, it may seem difficult to apply Scrum in your environment. There are many questions. What about the existing governance? How to deal with detailed budgets and year plans? How should you use Scrum when working times and workplaces are flexible?

It's always possible to find reasons why something can't be done. Don't focus on that. Instead, focus on what does work. Fast working results that make customers happy are always valuable. Work towards achieving that. Use the available space you have to maneuver towards making Scrum a success in your environment. Once you've shown it works, it will be much easier to expand beyond the first team.

This is typical for Scrum: focus on what can be done and learn to be successful at that as fast as possible.

"Man, you look tired!"

"Yeah, I didn't sleep well last night."

"How come?"

"Well, it's maddening. I'm so extremely overwhelmed at work, doing many separate different things every day that I'm completely exhausted when I come home at night."

"Wouldn't that make you sleep well?"

"Yeah, you'd think. It's not that I don't sleep, but I keep waking up around 2 am and after that I can't get back to sleep."

"Are you getting stressed about things?"

"Well, not so much getting stressed. It's more that all sorts of things go through my mind. Like, I suddenly remember I forgot to do something, or that I start thinking about what I want to get done the next day. Then I start thinking about these things and can't get back to sleep. This has been going on for a few weeks now."

"To me it seems like you're doing too much at once, not finishing most of it, discovering new things that need to get done along the way and are trying to manage all this in your mind. Am I right?"

"Sounds about right. Why?"

"You know I work using Scrum, right?"

"Yeah, so? I'm busy enough as it is. It's not exactly like I'm looking for more!"

"That's not what I mean. I'd like to help you with making a list."

"A list?"

"Yeah, right now you're doing so much at once you're losing sight of the overall picture, forget to do half you set out to do and lie awake at night thinking about it. We'll make a list and order the items on their priority with the most important one on top. Then we'll write "To Do" above this list and we'll have effectively cleared your mind from remembering what you need to do. Agreed?"

"I guess so. What if I find out at night I forgot something?"

"Put a stack of empty notes on your nightstand. If you wake up and think of something, write it on a note and you won't have to think of it again until morning."

"Is that it?"

"Well, no. We'll also make a column called "Doing" and a column called "Done". From then on it's your job to keep the board up-to-date. This is important because then and only then can you completely clear your mind from this. Because of this, your nights will be a lot more relaxing. Can you do that?"

"Yes, sure I can do that. When can we make this board?"

"I'm free right now. The sooner you clear your head and regain sight of the overall picture, the sooner you'll feel rested. So what do you say? Shall we do it immediately?"

"Great. I'll make the first note: "Make board". I'll put it in the 'Doing' column immediately!"

"Joker!"

How to apply Scrum in an existing (plan-driven) organization?

Focus on what can be done and not on what can't. There's always room to maneuver and make something happen. In the end, it's about creating a working result with a group of people and a bag of money. It's easy to come up with reasons why you shouldn't start with Scrum in a plan-driven environment. If you don't want to do something, you can always find reasons that justify not doing it. Focusing on everything that can't be done isn't very helpful.

Even so, in plan-driven environments there's much opportunity. The overall situation is still the same: everything changes, the market is dynamic, users don't know what they want, and the technology keeps surprising you. No matter how difficult, the need for short iterations and working results exists in any dynamic environment. If you can help a team be successful in such a setting, while being predictable, you'll eventually get the attention and means needed to change things. Usually it's possible to make room for a first Scrum team within a project. Starting out in a project that is completely stuck, too late, too expensive, and overall in a bad state can be an excellent way to get started. Something needs to change in that project anyway, so why not start working in short iterations, while focusing on providing value to the customer and producing a finished product at the end of each Sprint?

If you start with Scrum in an existing plan-driven organization, you always have to deal with dependencies. It just seems hard to stick to Scrum in an environment with a release calendar, strict waterfall processes, document-intensive methods, and a push for strictly controlled governance. Try to manage dependencies with others outside of the Sprint. When you need help of others because they have certain competencies or do necessary work for you, try to get them to finish the work first before you incorporate it into a Sprint. That's a sure way to keep them off the critical path. Another option is to temporarily add these people to the Scrum team. If you do this, get them to put their other activities on the Sprint Backlog as well.

This way they'll only work on items on the Sprint Backlog and, who knows, your Scrum team might be able to help them with their work so they have more time available to help you.

You'll wonder, what about everything that's stopping me? How do I deal with everything that works using a waterfall approach? Again, the answer is simple. What's possible? What can be applied? Focus on that. Regard everything that's blocking or hindering you as an impediment. Order the impediments based on their impact and work through them one by one. What was it again? How do you eat an elephant? Yes, exactly, bite by bite. So how do you deal with dependencies? Exactly, step by step!

One of the easiest things to take on first is "visualizing the workflow". Do this by demonstrating that Scrum teams are able to deliver a working result every two weeks. Put these results on a timeline, with concrete planned results for nearby Sprints and rougher estimates for Sprints that are further out. Adding external deadlines to this timeline makes upcoming problems visible quickly. Many people will claim that all this information was already available but putting the information highly visible on a wall adds an extra dimension to it. It's a social object that can be touched and passionately debated. This often results in surprisingly human and simple solutions to seemingly insurmountable problems.

What about the current procedures and roles?

Even in strict PRINCE2-driven organizations, adopting Scrum can be valuable. Don't immediately dismiss PRINCE2 or start working around it. Also, don't immediately refuse to report function points if this is mandatory in your organization. Instead, work within the existing boundaries and show how things can be done better. In the beginning, managing the contradictions between old and new, plan-driven and agile will be mostly your responsibility. Therefore, do workshops with stakeholders and end users, show working results, work together to make the results even better, and adapt when necessary.

So, if you aren't allowed to start without a Project Initiation Document, then you have to accept that for now. The same goes when you aren't allowed to show results to users until the very end. First demonstrate you can be successful and deliver reliable results within the existing boundaries. When you've managed this, it's time to step by step expand these boundaries. In a strict plan-driven environment, it's not fair to relax the rules first and then learn how to make Scrum a success with trial and error. In such an environment, people usually overreact to any mistake, so be careful that you don't provoke an intervention that will reaffirm the existing rules and make them even stricter.

Large organizations need procedures to steer in a certain direction. The *Scrum Guide* is excellent but usually insufficient to form the basis for a large implementation process or to anchor a large corporation. These are some examples: Scrum doesn't define a project leader but many organizations employ many PRINCE2-schooled project leaders. What are these people going to do? Scrum aims to avoid comprehensive documentation. But large organizations are used to producing this. What exactly should these organizations document from now on? Business Domain Architecture, Global Requirements, Functional Design, Software Architecture Document, Application Deployment Plan etc.? Which of these should they continue to produce? We only want to document to most essential things, but what will we say when an oversight body asks for certain documents? While the learning process is crucial to developing your own best practices, isn't a certain structure still needed when Scrum is applied on a larger scale?

General answers to these questions don't exist. What we do know is that when you start small it will be clear much sooner what you need and what the best way of working is for you. You'll learn more from acting than from thinking about it. Having said this, it's often also not very effective to change everything at once. So try to maneuver within the existing roles and procedures for now and work from there. Change one thing, monitor, and observe, then change another thing.

How about project budgets and year plans?

Using Scrum initially seems to rule out working with budgets and year plans. These are popular steering instruments in many organizations. So we'd like to know, how can we use these things while using Scrum?

First of all, a budget or year plan is inaccurate by definition. It's created in advance, which is the moment your knowledge is minimal. This is true whether you're using Scrum or not. Such plans and budgets only offer false security to base decisions on. This doesn't mean they're totally useless, but regarding them as steering instruments or the ultimate truth isn't a good idea either.

At the same time, it's often too big a leap to jump to "we won't make a plan, we'll see what we'll end up with, but we'll focus on producing the most value in two week periods". This is understandable. The management of nearly every company in which Scrum is introduced has difficulties with comprehending Scrum. Firstly, year plans don't have open-endings. Secondly, you have to know in advance whether you need to scale up your capacity (more Scrum teams) because scaling up takes time.

So, we need estimations in advance, on all three levels: project, product, and company. Not planning anything in advance doesn't work either. In the end of the day, you'll need a Product Backlog to know what direction you want to go. And this needs to be planned. Further out it's acceptable for this planning to be more rough, but that's enough to estimate the amount of work that needs to be done and, therefore, also the budget. If you know how much it costs to perform one Sprint and you know the budget, you can easily calculate how many Sprints you can afford.

What if the estimation is still too vague? You simply use the first few Sprints to make clear what can and what cannot be done and how much this will cost. The first Sprint clears up a lot: is the idea valuable enough, is it technically feasible, is the team up to the task, and is the idea feasible within the time and budgetary restrictions? By quickly making a working product, these questions are rapidly answered. Making plans and detailed specifications in advance also costs time and money. Generally, the results of the first few Sprints paint a much better picture and are even cheaper and quicker! Also, if it becomes clear that the result is not achievable, it is better to cancel the project rather than continue wasting money.

The above is true for year plans also. Work these out in themes and what you want to achieve. How to realize this can be worked out later. By doing this, the amount of time and money and the number of Sprints you need is clear.

Flexible office spaces, part-timers, and flexible working times versus stable teams

Working with flexible working times and locations is becoming more and more common. Nowadays "New World of Work" is also gaining popularity. New World of Work is mainly known because of the flexible office spaces it prescribes. When you come into the office, you look for a place to work that matches the needs you have at that moment. An expansion on this that is often seen is working from home to avoid wasting time in traffic. Next to this, the number of part-time jobs is increasing. Flexible working times are also common these days.

How does all this work with Scrum? Doesn't Scrum prescribe stable teams, full-time presence, daily coordination, short communication lines, and joint team spaces? Don't these concepts rule each other out?

At a first glance is does appear so, but when you think about it a bit more, you'll see that all these aspects are about self-organization and responsibility for the end result. Because we focus on the result, we don't need to focus as much on defining a strict process. Placing trust in competent people and their intrinsic motivation to achieve the best results they can is a core principle. The team itself is responsible for making promises about what they'll deliver and sticking to those promises. People are considered mature enough to do their job and support is coordinated within the team. Next to this, coordination and transparency are important pillars.

Define the result and steer towards achieving this result. Then, let the team organize itself to make it a reality. You'll see that working times are arranged, team spaces are created, and arrangements are made regarding absence from Scrum Meetings and so on. The team will find its own way to make it possible to achieve the results in an effective way.

So, in short: stable teams in Scrum and flexible working arrangements are not mutually exclusive. In fact, they reinforce each other. A team simply needs the space to arrange these things to be able to become a self-organizing team.

How can you adapt Scrum to your organization (or adapt your organization to be agile)?

Don't! Scrum is a complete system and the different aspects are tightly connected. Whatever you do and however you apply it, be sure to apply all aspects. Do you only want to apply some aspects because they seem useful in isolation? By all means, do so! But you won't reap all the benefits you could by applying them all. Remember, Scrum as a whole is more than the sum of its parts. So make sure you always have the following:

1. **Sprints** – *Short iterations of static duration*
   Divide the available time to create a constant rhythm. By doing so, you'll develop an intuition for what's feasible. Iterations of one or two weeks are common, less than one month is essential.

2. **Product owner** – *One decision maker who orders on value*
   Choose the desired order of the results. Appoint one person to be responsible and allowed to do this. To be able to do this correctly, that person needs to gather all stakeholders.

3. **Product Backlog** – *One transparent wish list*
   There should only be one wish list. The mutual priorities can change, so make the list flexible. A way to make this clear is by using post-its or index cards.

4. **Development Team** – *Stable cross-functional teams with no side-jobs*
   The work is done by a team that encompasses all competencies to implement everything on the Product Backlog. The team only works on one list and this is a joint effort of the entire team.

5. **Sprint Planning** – *The people who do the work make the estimates and do the planning themselves*
   To make results predictable, the work should be estimated and planned by the people doing the actual work. Planning and estimating is only done in detail for one Sprint in advance.

6. **Sprint Backlog** – *Use a task board to share the current state of the work*
   The work that a team will carry out in a certain period should be made clear in a list of tasks. The state of these tasks changes as work is being carried out on these tasks. The team members maintain this state themselves.

7. **Product Increment** – *Finish what you start*
   Everything should be a step towards the creation of a working result. So, focus on constantly finishing what you start in a way that it provides value to your customer.

8. **Definition-of-Done** – *Decide when something is done*
   When something is done isn't always clear to everyone. Make this explicit with the team and the decision maker and make a checklist with the requirements for work to be done.

9. **Daily Scrum** – *Coordinate progress and prospects very frequently*
   To make sure you always know where you stand and whether

people need help, you should coordinate very frequently. This should be done at least daily.

10. **Sprint Review** – *Clearly communicate what you are doing currently and what you are going to do*
    To make sure that you're doing the right thing, you should show the customer the result of your actions at least once every Sprint. By doing so, you'll receive feedback and slowly discover what's needed.

11. **Sprint Retrospective** – *Learn something from every iteration*
    Make sure you learn by doing. To make sure you do, reserve some time at the end of every iteration to discuss what should change to make the next iteration better. In every iteration, at least one improvement should be made.

12. **Product Backlog Refinement** – *Make the work clear before you start*
    To be able to work in a predictable fashion, you should only select work that you can finish within the Sprint. Therefore, you should regularly look at the work with the entire team, clarify it further, and break it up to make it feasible.

13. **Time-Boxed Meetings** – *Time-box everything*
    When you're coordinating or consulting, you're not adding value directly. Meetings should never take longer than planned. It should be clear in advance how long a meeting will take and the meeting should always finish on time.

14. **Scrum Master** – *Arrange for a process mentor*
    Because all this is very different from most normal environments, there should be someone who helps guide the process and plays the role of coach to make sure the process improves every iteration. So this person is both the protector of the process and coach of the team in one.

What should you do?

- Find out what is possible in your organization.
- Don't waste energy pursuing things you can't (yet) accomplish.
- Guide your environment step-by-step.
- Try to use the budget for making a detailed plan for creating a real first version of the end product.
- Visualize the workflow with post-its on the wall (what's the most valuable?).
- Leverage flexible working conditions to allow teams to self-organize.
- Don't adapt Scrum to your organization from the get-go. *It's a complete system with tightly interrelated aspects.*
- Remember that it's easier to learn by doing something than it is by just thinking about it.

WHAT DOES SCRUM COST AND WHAT ARE THE RETURNS?

THE EXPECTED RETURN ON INVESTMENT (ROI) OF SCRUM IS USUALLY AROUND 1:10

— CHAPTER 6 —

WHAT DOES SCRUM COST AND WHAT ARE THE RETURNS?

Calculating the real ROI is difficult but the available data show that making $10 on every invested dollar is feasible. Of course, this is only an indication and actual results will depend on the conditions of the specific setting. Our own experience confirms this rough estimate.

The average cost for introducing Scrum into an organization is approximately $7,500 for every employee for training and guidance. With an ROI of 1:10, the realistic return on this investment is $75,000 per employee per year. This doesn't include all the other advantages like transparency, motivation, or customer satisfaction, and many more. However, real hyper-productivity is difficult to achieve in practice. But this is primarily because teams don't apply Scrum correctly or aren't enabled to do so in their work environment. So assistance and the right vision from management are crucial for achieving a good ROI.

The most important added value of Scrum, however, is the increase in agility. In the current market, it's essential to be able to respond to change quickly. The practical costs of *not* being able to change directions are very high. Sometimes you'll even end up paying the ultimate price.

Or like Darwin said, "*It is not the strongest of the species that survive, nor the most intelligent, but the one most responsive to change*".

"Yesterday I talked to our comptroller about our Scrum results. Do you know what he asked?"

"Well?"

"He asked: 'What's the return from using Scrum?' And do you know what? I didn't really have an answer for that. Surely, everything we do should make money."

"Yes, but it does, right? If everyone is feeling better and the customer's more satisfied that everything's going much better than before. What else does the comptroller want?"

"Well simply: to see money! Everyone has done training and Product Owners are freed from doing other work. They only contribute indirectly now. Add to that the two external Agile consultants we have to pay. These are all costs we are making. I think the comptroller's entirely right for asking what return we get on all these expenses. I have a general feeling in what aspects we're getting a return on our money, but I don't have actual figures. Do you?"

"Well, I think it's rubbish. It's clear for everyone we're doing much better now than before. All our people and customers are more satisfied. Don't you think that's profitable? I could fit that business case on a napkin!"

"Well show me! Spell it out on a napkin for me please!"

"Okay, sure. Let's keep it simple. I'll focus on two things: more satisfied customers and more frequent releases. We service a hundred customers with an average turnover of 200k, right?"

"Just about. That won't be off by much."

"So last year about 10% of our customers switched to a competitor. That's two million in turnover. In the last year no customers switched and ten new ones joined us. Let's estimate a conservative net margin of

20%. This amounts to 400k profit in this year alone. Agreed?"

"Seems credible and conservative."

"All right, but that isn't it. Next to this we deliver new software every month instead of every year. The average savings on a change is at least 1%. Now those savings aren't released yearly but monthly! So we're twelve times as fast. So every improvement's now valuable about ten times quicker! This is also easily 200k a year. At least! In this year alone using Scrum has earned us half a million. And what did adopting Scrum cost us again?"

"I don't have exact numbers but the comptroller mentioned $50.000 in trainings and consultancy. I don't think this includes the invested time of our own people, though."

"So we're done calculating then right? On a cash-in cash-out basis we've achieved a ROI of 1,000% and if we include our own invested time we've at the very least achieved a result higher than 1:5. We've made at least 5 dollars for every dollar we've invested. Do we ever achieve results this good?"

"I think you're right! Could you work this out on a spreadsheet for me? Next week we'll have a two-day gathering of the entire management and I'm going to present the Scrum session."

"OK, sure. But can I come and present it myself? Individuals and interactions remember?"

"Ha ha ha, yeah, you're right. I'll make sure you're invited!"

What is the Return on Investment of Scrum?

Although Scrum is very popular and many organizations have adopted it, the available data on the costs and returns are still very limited. The most recent Agile Survey by Version One shows that 90% of the respondents are much better able to adapt to changing priorities and that transparency is vastly improved. But how much money does this make?

David Rico[1] investigates ROI based on publications and uses this to build simulation models. His results show positive results as he published a 1:7 ROI for Scrum, 1:19 for Agile, and 1:32 for Extreme Programming (sometimes in combination with Scrum). The generalizability of the models Rico uses is, however, not generally accepted in the scientific community. Next to this, these models are biased towards methods targeting individual tasks over methods targeting teams and organizations. Having said this, the predictions are indicative but very promising. Having something concrete always beats having nothing.

The Standish Group published data showing that the success chances of projects are three times higher than waterfall projects, and the chance of a failing project is three times lower than with waterfall. Depending on your organization, these figures can be used to calculate indicators of the true ROI. Jeff Sutherland (the co-creator of Scrum) has said he believes a ROI of 1,000% to be realistic and a budget of 400,000 dollars to be a sufficient starting point for a department of 60 people. You don't need to spend the entire budget before you start reaping the rewards! Straight from the first Sprint, the positive results will start to appear.

Our own experiences match the above viewpoints. Hard data may be lacking, but in our experience, the general ROI is in the order of magnitude of 1:10. Therefore, assume a budget of approximately $7,500 per employee in costs for training, guidance, and coaching.

---

1   http://davidfrico.com/agile-book.htm

Based on the expected ROI of 1:10, a return of about $75,000 per year is a realistic expectation.

Importantly, this investment doesn't need to be made upfront. This can be avoided by working in phases (for example team by team or department by department). The profit that's made in the first team can be used to realize the adoption of Scrum in the next one. This allows you to immediately prove the legitimacy of the business case in practice. Another added benefit is that this approach increases the overall ROI. So again, working in phases (iteratively) is advantageous.

To sum up, in every organization we go to, at some point there's a discussion about costs, returns, and ROI of Scrum. Therefore, it's essential to make the costs and returns measurable and tangible. An expected ROI of 1:10 and a budget or $7,500 per employee are valid starting points.

The five most important benefits of Scrum

Many benefits are reported in practice: satisfied employees and customers, short delivery times, flexibility, higher quality, shorter learning cycles, etc. At the same time, these benefits aren't free and it's not guaranteed they'll be realized. The five most important benefits of Scrum we focus on in practice are:

1. **Growth in agility.** The extent in which change is easier and cheaper and also how flexible you are to respond to your customers' needs. Using an index it's possible to calculate how mature your organization is measured on an agile scale. To which extent do you deliver working and tested software to your customers in a successful way with self-organizing team? Does this happen faster and faster? Are your customers increasingly satisfied?

2. **Shorter release cycles.** Measuring the time between idea and delivery (the lead time), the time between deliveries (the cycle time), or simply the number of deliveries, we can see

how big this advantage is. Software that is done but not yet released isn't valuable. Therefore, how fast things are released is a metric that indicates the monetary return.

3. **Higher business value/productivity.** The extent to which teams produce value is an indicator of the value of Scrum. Value is attributed to wishes on the backlog and the productivity of teams can be expressed in the delivered business value per employee per year.

4. **Improved predictability.** The extent to which teams deliver predictable results and are able to generate value when this is expected is an important benefit. The amount of deadlines or release dates that are missed can be used to determine the cost/return of Scrum. In particular the reduction of problems with quality and the automatic testing of quality are important.

5. **Customer and employee satisfaction.** At the end of the day, it's about satisfied customers through happy employees. It's possible to express satisfaction in numbers (for example NPS: Net Promoter Score) that are convertible to financial value to the organization.

Each of these benefits is quantifiable and either directly or indirectly convertible to financial value. This will differ between organizations and settings. We do recommend making this financial value measurable and tangible. In the end, it's necessary to determine ROI. When you know what the returns are of something, you know what costs are acceptable as well.

The four reasons why Scrum results in a strong growth in productivity

Scrum promises fast delivery of working software every 30 days or less, usually two weeks, which satisfies users and creates value. Scrum is able to deliver productivity growth because of four reasons that each results in at least a doubling of productivity on its own. At least a doubling. So by chaining these four improvements ($2 \times 2 \times 2 \times 2 = 16$), a tenfold increase is easily achieved and a twentyfold increase is feasible. So the potential of an enormous increase in productivity seems justified.

1. **With Scrum you truly finish work.** Each Sprint results in a working and tested result for end users. Thus, rework is prevented, mistakes are found and solved more quickly, and changing direction is made possible. To make sure everything is truly finished Scrum teams use a list of criteria that need to be met for work to be done. This list is called the "Definition-of-Done". At the same time, Scrum requires a big change to be able to deliver every Sprint. This requires teams to truly work as a team and not just stay within their core competencies. By truly finishing the work, the team is more focused and creates better quality. Because of this a doubling of productivity is feasible.

2. **With Scrum you start with the most valuable.** A Sprint primarily results in the things that are the most valuable. To do this, Scrum defines the role of Product Owner. A Product Owner knows what is valuable and can make the right choices. Because of a focus on the most important things only, teams will finish early. It's important to note that good is good enough. This will more than double the productivity of team. Teams won't waste time on things that are less valuable.

3. **With Scrum you focus on what is feasible.** Since Scrum teams need to deliver a working result every two weeks, they only take on work that can be completely finished within a two-week period. The teams only work on things they're sure they can complete. This easily doubles the productivity. The paradoxical thing is that teams that plan less than others, but only plan that which is clear, get more things done. To make this easier, some Scrum teams choose to work with a list of criteria that determine whether a piece of work is clear enough. This list is called the *"Definition of Ready"* (DoR).

4. **With Scrum teams your productivity will continuously improve.** Scrum teams should improve every Sprint. Creating stable teams that improve every Sprint at least doubles the productivity as well.

In practice, we see that many Scrum teams are struggling with these things. We encounter many teams that don't deliver working and tested results every Sprint. Some teams don't use a Definition-of-Done or don't stick to it. We also encounter many teams without a Product Owner or with a Product Owner without sufficient authority or time. We encounter teams that take on work that is too big and not clear enough. Furthermore, many organizations struggle to allow teams to be stable. Finally, many teams don't really have a chance to improve because of impediments outside of their control.

So, saying you've adopted Scrum is easy; actually doing it is hard. In practice, we see that only about one in ten teams manages to become hyper-productive. Most teams do manage to double their productivity.

Facts don't lie

Large consultancy agencies such as Gartner, Standish, and McKinsey recommend to stop working in a plan-driven fashion using a waterfall approach, but instead to use an agile approach.

The Gartner report is very explicit in this: *"The End of the Waterfall as We Know It"*.

Furthermore, the Standish Group has shown that the chance of success is three times higher when using an agile approach compared to a plan-driven approach. Of course you can question the legitimacy of the data, but you can also wonder how much data you need. Standish even states, *"Agile is the universal remedy for software development project failure"*.

Next to this, Scrum is the most used agile approach. The 7th Annual State of Agile shows that 70% of companies that use agile apply Scrum (either pure or in a hybrid version).

This doesn't mean Scrum is the solution to all your problems. Quite the contrary. Of course there are situations in which you can perfectly plan in advance. In those cases, the added value of Scrum is far lower. Scrum is also not extremely useful for work that is repetitive and with little or no outside influences. Having said this, most of what we do is done for the first time. Most of what we do has a strong IT component. Most of what we do changes due to new insights. Most of what we do involves a dynamic and unpredictable market.

Most of what we do is perfectly suited for Scrum!

What should you do?

- Assume a transition budget of roughly $7.500 per team member is needed for training and guidance.
- Explicitly choose your goals in adopting Scrum. Make the returns measurable. Consider all other benefits to be "nice-to-haves".
- Calculate the ROI of the introduction of Scrum based on the cost and the return.
- Calculate the past results and compare them with the results when using Scrum.
- Adopt Scrum in phases so you can use the profit of the first team to pay for the next team.

HOW DO YOU ADOPT SCRUM?

USE SCRUM TO ADOPT SCRUM: STEP BY STEP AND DOING THE MOST VALUABLE THING FIRST. YOU CAN START RIGHT NOW: JUST DO IT!

— CHAPTER 7 —

HOW DO YOU ADOPT SCRUM?

The best tool in adopting Scrum is Scrum itself. This makes sense because Scrum is particularly suited for complex projects. So, use the rhythm dictated by Sprints and a transparent list of tasks (Backlog) to adopt Scrum. Choose a rhythm that matches the speed of adoption in your organization. Just like for regular sprint teams, the shorter the Sprints, the better, so choose Sprints of one or two weeks if possible.

Go through the normal rhythm of Planning, Daily Scrum, Review, and Retrospectives. Also make a transparent Sprint Backlog. Demonstrate that Scrum is being used to start using Scrum. It's also advisable to make a dashboard that shows how the adoption of Scrum in the teams is going and what results are being achieved in the form of KPIs. Put this dashboard on the wall as an example of transparency.

To summarize, *Don't just talk the talk but also walk the walk!*

"We should first make a Scrum handbook."

"Excuse me?"

"Before we start adopting Scrum, we need a handbook."

"Why?"

"Isn't it obvious? Our teams need guidance and can't figure it all out on their own. Moreover, we can't afford to end up with forty different Scrum variants. Then we have to spend a year more to set it all straight afterwards. No, we really need a handbook."

"Wait a minute. You're saying two things at once now. Firstly, you want to help the teams with becoming Scrum teams, right?"

"Yes."

"Next, to that you want a uniform implementation so everyone applies Scrum in the same fashion, correct?"

"Yes!"

"But we already have the Scrum Guide! The Scrum Guide's uniform, maintained by Jeff Sutherland himself, and is also available for free in all languages! We can download it easily from www.scrumguides.org. What else do you need?"

"Come on, you know better than that! We need our own custom version. Do you really think the general Scrum Guide is directly applicable in our setting?"

"Oh, is that what you mean. What do you think we should customize?"

"I don't know. Start a group to figure it out."

"But if you don't know, what makes you think others will? I think we first need to learn how we can best apply Scrum in our organization. We are at the very start of our experience with Scrum. At the moment we know the least. It would be foolish to make this kind of decisions now. That would mean there's nothing left to learn for us."

"I think you have another view on this. What do you suggest?"

"Well, why don't we allow ourselves to learn? Why don't we use Scrum as described in the Scrum Guide for the first two or three teams? The experience we'll gain by that will be valuable when we adopt Scrum in the teams after that. Doesn't that seem like a better approach?"

"Hmmmm... seems to make sense. But what kind of assistance can we offer the first teams? We can't just give them the Scrum Guide, can we?"

"You know what? I'll make a presentation in our own corporate style. But the content of the presentation will be the exact content of the Scrum Guide. On the second sheet I'll leave room for best practices and examples. We can use this space for our own ideas and experiences. What do you think? Is this a good idea?"

"Seems straightforward enough. Let's do it! Do you want to take the lead on this one?"

"No problem!"

The first ten steps towards an agile organization

There isn't much that needs to be done before starting with Scrum. In the end, Scrum is only a different way of organizing the work. It might not be immediately apparent, but basically Scrum is just a GTD (Getting Things Done) for teams. It makes organizing the work in teams easier. Nothing should stop you from starting right away.

Having said this, it isn't always appropriate to start right away with a large transition towards Scrum. We've seen that in many cases people need a roadmap. An obvious roadmap, based on years of experience with large transitions, is the following:

1. **Organize an agile awareness session and a Scrum introduction workshop.** Begin with one or more agile awareness sessions and Scrum workshops. These sessions can be led by an (external) Scrum consultant or Agile coach. These sessions help people with thinking in terms of iterations, agility, and prioritizing on value. They present Scrum in more detail and work towards an initial list of things that need to be done to start with Scrum.

2. **Organize agile coaching.** A transition towards an agile way of working shouldn't be done with trial and error alone. It's a good idea to bring external expertise to help. We've developed "*the A team*" concept to decide what expertise you need:

    - an agile strategy coach, who mainly acts on the management level,
    - an Agile coach, who is mainly involved with the transition team and middle management,
    - one or more team coaches, who help to get the Scrum teams started,
    - one or more technical coaches, who mainly support things such as automating quality control.

Not all members of the A team are needed on a full-time basis. Depending on the scale, their work is limited to a few hours or a few days.

3. **Organize a management workshop and determine the members of the steering committee.** A management workshop is a good way to start. Depending on the exact situation, this workshop could be placed earlier on the roadmap. If no Agility Owner has been appointed, this is done in this workshop. Next to this, this workshop is used to determine the initial Transition Backlog and which of the workshop participants will form the steering committee.

4. **Form a Scrum transition team and determine its rhythm.** Form a transition team that should include the Agility Owner, the Agile coaches, and a sample of the employees. Make sure the team isn't too large: it should never have more than nine members and the most effective teams have five through seven members. The team determines its own rhythm usually around a month, as it takes a lot of effort to effect organizational change. Having a steady rhythm makes things easier. It can be difficult to plan in the beginning, but after a few Sprints everyone's used to it. The steering committee should be invited to the Sprint Reviews of the transition team and plays the role of owner. In the Sprint Review, the Transition Backlog should be reviewed by the Agility Owner based on the feedback.

5. **Determine the Transition Backlog, the KPIs, and reporting.** In a half-a-day workshop, the transition team should create the Transition Backlog. The Agility Owner prioritizes this backlog. Next to this, the KPIs of the transition are determined. When is the introduction of Scrum successful? What should we measure to determine

this? These KPIs should be placed on a dashboard used to make the progress transparent.

6. **Determine the composition of the Scrum teams and choose an introduction sequence.** It's also common to use the previous step to decide the order in which the Scrum teams are formed. It isn't always immediately clear what the composition of the teams should be. Remember that it's an important separate step to determine the makeup of the Scrum teams and the order in which they're formed.

7. **Organize soapbox sessions for management (why, how, and what).** Too often this step is forgotten. Many organizations start with a large-scale rollout without introducing Scrum properly to everyone. Don't assume everyone just gets the how, what, and why of such a transition. Therefore, it's important that the leaders of the organization (usually management) take the stand and explain this. Explicitly communicate why you're doing this, what steps are going to be taken, and what this will mean to everyone.

8. **Form the Scrum teams and celebrate success.** Subsequently, the Scrum teams are formed. Usually, this takes a few months per team. The most important thing is that the teams do the forming themselves, so the guidance of the Scrum coach follows the rhythm: demonstrate, participate, and watch. We recommend for the teams to start with one-week iterations. By doing so, the rate of learning is improved and people in these teams quickly get used to thinking: what can we do within a Sprint? Next to this, it's essential to emphasize and celebrate successes. Put the spotlight on teams that are successful. Management should attend Sprint Reviews. Celebrate with champagne if a team achieves something extraordinary. In short, be energetic in

the face of success and make sure things are learned in the case of failure.

9. **Train Scrum Masters, Product Owners, and Development Teams.** Starting a Scrum team begins with training that includes determining the Product Backlog and agreeing the Definition-of-Done (checklist). Depending on the organization, this kick-off training takes a day or a few days. Immediately after, the team starts with the first Sprint. Next to this, everyone needs to be trained for their new role. This is usually done by doing a certified training. It's best to do this training after experiencing a few Sprints. This results in everyone attending the training with practical experience and a number of concrete questions.

10. **Secure and anchor Scrum in the system and structures.** The next stage is to embed the new way of working in the organization's systems and structures. Especially in large organizations, governance is very important. It's recommended to start a number of Scrum teams *before* deciding on the Scrum governance to be followed. It would be a waste of time and effort to work on this beforehand only to find out it doesn't work in practice. When thinking of structures, remember personnel policies, reviews, bonuses, and salaries. Make sure these align with the focus on value and working towards concrete results as a team.

The above steps seem to resemble a waterfall, right? This seems contradictory to the values of Scrum. Even so, in practice, people need something to refer to when adopting Scrum. It would be easy to say, "just get a few agile coaches and then everything will work itself ou'". However, the above roadmap isn't a plan that should be followed step by step and to the letter. Before you reach the end, a new dynamic will present itself in the rhythm of the Sprints. At that point, you can stop following the roadmap. Until that happens, the roadmap is there to refer to and for support.

Six choices for team focus

An important step when starting with Scrum is determining team composition. To be able to do this in an informed way, it's important to decide the focus of the team. Will the team focus on a customer or group of customers? Will it focus on a subsystem or does it perform a business function such as sales?

A rule of thumb is that the higher the value to the customer that can be achieved the better. Keeping this in mind, a number of possibilities for composing teams come to mind. Beware! The options we discuss are ordered from low flexibility to high and from indirect customer value to direct customer value. Try to determine the best fit for your organization. In a plan-driven organization, Option 1 might be easiest to achieve, and it's also the least effective. Constantly work towards the bottom of the list of options.

1. **Teams with a silo focus.** These are teams that only take the role of one link in the chain. They work in their own isolated silo, which is only one link in the chain. Examples include a marketing team following Scrum, a sales team, and a development department that doesn't do testing but instead delivers an untested product to the testing department. The effect of choosing this option is that only one link in the chain is made agile, but that customer value is still created by the entire chain. Having said this, this option can be a good way to get started with Scrum and to find out what it's all about.

2. **Teams with a technology focus.** These are teams with high fragmentation. Examples are database teams and Siebel teams. Such teams deliver components that usually aren't subsystems. The largest disadvantage of this composition is

that it's hard to steer towards valuable results. Also, it's often hard to integrate the work of such teams. Because of this, it can still take months to deliver the wishes of customers. How agile is it then? Sometimes, this composition is the only way to start with Scrum, but try to move on to a subsequent option as soon as possible.

3. **Teams with a sub-system focus.** These teams work on parts of products. The teams depend on the work of other teams for delivering the actual product. With this kind of team, integration is always a difficult problem. In this team composition, the creation of value is often still indirect and it requires intensive coordination with other teams to create an integrated product that is ready for the customer to use. An example is the division in a front-end and back-end team. The customer only sees the front-end, but the value is created by the combination of front- and back-end. This is also not a great team composition but sometimes there is no other way. Again, it's advisable to work towards team compositions further down this list as soon as possible.

4. **Teams with a product focus.** These teams distinguish themselves by working towards adding value in the form of a product (for more than one customer). The Product Owner is responsible for converting the wishes of all customers towards a prioritization on the backlog. This kind of team composition is the typical way in which most organizations start out with Scrum: teams with cross-functional competences that together work on one product. It's also a common way of working with Scrum in companies with a strong division between business and IT. The largest disadvantage of this way of working is that the team members themselves have little insight in the customer value they deliver.

5. **Teams with a customer focus.** These teams directly service one or more customers. The team is responsible for all the work that is needed to provide value to a specific customer. The set of required competences in these teams is larger than all the types of teams discussed above but smaller than the set needed for a full business focus, discussed below. Sales is an example of something that is still taken care of outside a customer-focused team. These teams have a difficult time if they service more than one customer. If this is the case, the Product Owner is also responsible for deciding the priority between servicing the different customers. This isn't always easy. If only one customer is serviced per team, it's easier and in that case, the role of Product Owner can sometimes be taken on by the customer. Next to this, it's difficult when the amount of work for a certain customer dries up or becomes less important. When this happens, the team might be doing the most valuable thing for this specific customer, but could create more value for another one.

6. **Teams with a full business focus.** These teams deliver business value in a certain area in a completely integrated fashion. They encompass all the skills necessary to create a solution from an idea to a concrete product that has value to a customer (or a customer's customer). These are fully cross-functional teams that provide a customer domain or full business proposition. This type of Scrum team basically functions as a miniature company. It takes care of everything, from market research and experiments to sales and delivery. This shares many aspects with the concept of "Lean Startup". It's often difficult to start with these teams immediately, but they are very agile and add direct and measurable value to the bottom line. If you can pull this off, do it!

When are you done with adopting Scrum?

Well, you never are. There's always room for improvement. And Scrum isn't transitive so it never stops either. Things do change after the initial introduction. The idea is that Scrum will become part of the organization, that the rhythm of self-improvement will become the steady heart rate of the organization. When this happens, the adoption of Scrum and the associated continuous improvement have become the primary process in the organization. Of course, this can take a while – at least a few years for most organizations.

Following the initial introduction, it's often a good idea to do a second round with all the Scrum coaches. Then the Scrum coaches will again visit every team to help them to improve, both in their achievements and in how they apply Scrum. Setting up guilds is part of this, but for more on that, see chapter 13 of this book about scaling Scrum.

After a while, the agile coaching can be phased out. The intensity of the first period is no longer necessary. Scrum teams should be able to stand on their own feet then and the Scrum Master will take on the majority of the coaching that is still needed. You will encounter problems in other parts of your organization because Scrum teams work much faster than non-Scrum teams. In addition, most Scrum teams don't take on the entire value chain up to and including the customer, so new problems arise, either in the Scrum teams or in the link behind them.

A big danger in the introduction of Scrum is being too plan-driven and forced about it. You can't waterfall into agile. With this, we mean that an organization doesn't take on Scrum on a trial-and-error basis but enforces it through control and compliance. This makes Scrum the goal and not the means to an end. Adopting Scrum in that fashion isn't effective and doesn't help grow an agile mindset. Please don't!

What KPIs help monitor the introduction of Scrum?

You determine what you're trying to achieve in the Transition Backlog. We've experienced that the following KPIs are valuable to monitor the process:

Before the overall transition to Scrum:
- number of formed Scrum teams and burn-down
- guidance and training effort and burn-down
- growth in agility or agility index or burn-up

For every Scrum team:
- extent to which a working result is delivered every Sprint conforming to the checklist
- extent to which work and delivery is predictable (norm: +/- 20%)
- extent to which the Scrum meetings are done and properly time-boxed
- extent to which the team intensively collaborates with the Product Owner
- extent to which the team collaborates internally (Work In Progress < team members)
- extent to which the team actively improves itself
- happiness of the customer (when appropriate)
- happiness of the team
- happiness of the Product Owner

For every Product Owner:
- extent to which the Product Owner is available, trained, and has the proper authority
- extent to which the Product Owner keeps his or her Product Backlog in order (the norm is a backlog that looks six months ahead and is estimated by the team)
- extent to which the Product Owner prioritizes the Product Backlog based on value

- extent to which sufficient work is ready to be included in a Sprint (work for two or three Sprints "Ready" is the norm)
- extent to which the Product Owner applies predictable results management (keeping the burn-up up-to-date)
- extent to which the Product Owner is in charge in the Sprint Review and invites stakeholders

For every Scrum Master:
- extent to which the *Scrum Master is available, trained, and in charge*
- extent to which the *Scrum Master monitors how well Scrum is being applied*
- extent to which the *Scrum Master actively seeks out and resolves impediments*
- extent to which the *Scrum Master realizes improvements inside and outside of the team*

What should you do?

- Plan the introduction of Scrum along the ten steps presented in this chapter.
- Consider this plan to be a starting point and for support.
- Adapt the plan when you discover things should be done differently.
- Make a conscious decision on how to focus the teams when constructing them.
- Actively work towards a stronger focus on customer value for these teams.
- Realize you're never done: when resolving one bottleneck, the next will present itself.
- Create a dashboard with KPIs for the adoption of Scrum.
- Make this dashboard visible to everyone and keep it up-to-date.

WHAT ARE COMMON PITFALLS WITH SCRUM?

THERE AREN'T ANY REAL PITFALLS WITH SCRUM, JUST A LOT OF OPPORTUNITIES TO LEARN BY TRIAL AND ERROR!

CHAPTER 8

WHAT ARE COMMON PITFALLS WITH SCRUM?

People regularly ask us, "Doesn't anything ever go wrong when starting with Scrum?" Of course it does! After all, everyone's doing it for the first time. It would be odd if everything went perfectly from the start. The title of this chapter gets down to the heart of the matter: Are you allowed to make mistakes? Is making mistakes acceptable in your organization? Are you allowed to learn? Processes with very long cycles, such as the waterfall approach, make it possible to make such large mistakes that the entire project fails. This is where the fear of making mistakes comes from. Short cycles result in small mistakes. If you trip and fall, it's easy to get up again, learn from your mistake, and move on. On to the next pitfall! With this attitude, pitfalls aren't a problem but a learning experience.

There are many of these learning opportunities (a.k.a. pitfalls) in Scrum. So make sure it's okay to trip when a pitfall come along. The most common pitfalls in Scrum are:

- fear of failure
- not being able to deal with transparency and openness
- experiencing the problems that are exposed as too painful
- managing Scrum teams in a controlling fashion
- making decisions on details that should be made by the Scrum teams
- not measuring the costs and returns of Scrum
- only measuring how happy everyone is
- only applying half of the Scrum practices
- adapting Scrum before having even started.

Make sure you encourage Scrum teams to resolve problems as they emerge. That way, you'll never have to worry about pitfalls.

"Listen up. A tennis buddy of mine also works with Scrum and it doesn't go so well even though they customized Scrum to match their situation."

"What did they customize?"

"Well, he told me they don't work with mixed teams. You know, with testers, developers and designers in one team."

"Cross-functional teams?"

"Yeah, that. They apply what they call the 'roof tile-model'."

"Roof tile-model?"

"Yeah, they put all the designers in one Scrum team and let them perform an entire Sprint. Then the work is passed to the developer Scrum team who work on it for a week and finally hand it over to the tester team. So each successive team effectively runs one Sprint behind the team before them."

"I've never heard of that. It happens more often that people make these bizarre customizations. Another common one is teams that are freaked out by the Daily Scrum. Because of that, they only do it once a week, preferably in long Sprints of at least six weeks. And they usually get away with that too."

"What do you mean?"

"Well, apparently their management accepts that teams don't abide to the Scrum agreements. These are very clear: every day a Daily Scrum of 15 minutes and Sprints of no longer than a month, but preferably shorter. If management accepts that those principles are undermined they shouldn't complain that things don't go very well either. You know what you should ask next time someone tells you he works with Scrum?"

"Well?"

"Ask him three questions.

1. Do you really have a working and tested result every four weeks or less?
2. Do you really deliver the things with the highest business value first?
3. Do you really work with stable teams who continuously improve their inner-processes?

Usually they'll look at you with a confused look because that's not what they're doing at all. And I wouldn't trust people who answer 'Yes!' to all these questions without reservations either."

"Why not?"

"Because it's hard. Doing those three things is really tricky. But, if you're able to pull it off you will be very flexible and results-oriented."

"You'll be agile!"

"Exactly!"

When does Scrum fail?

Learning to apply Scrum is tricky and it doesn't always work on the first try. Usually, something will go wrong at some point. But is it really a pitfall if it just doesn't work on the first try? Does this make it a failure?

Not being allowed to make mistakes and learn from them is probably the biggest pitfall in adopting Scrum. Environments that aren't able to deal with the pain experienced when something goes wrong have a hard time starting with Scrum. This is because people adapt their behavior to avoid pain or to feel pleasure. Therefore, there is often resistance to the introduction of Scrum in environments in which making mistakes is experienced as painful.

How well is your organization able to deal with mistakes? How important is it to be able to blame someone? Is it acceptable to learn by discovery?

Failure is good when you're trying to learn. However, it can be a big and painful step. Not just for you, but also to others in your organization. This is why you often hear that Scrum requires a change in culture.

Sometimes we tell people: Scrum is like your mother-in-law: she enters you home and points out everything that's wrong, but doesn't do anything to fix it. On the other hand, if you're in an environment that can't handle the openness of mistakes and problems, this could be another reason for Scrum. Eventually you'll develop a thick skin!

In all the years we've been helping companies with Scrum, we've learned that all arguments used against Scrum are even stronger arguments against a fully planned process. This is true for all pitfalls discussed in this chapter. It's better to use a process that exposes these pitfalls so you can improve.

Learning is the only way to get better at what you do, so *prepare to fail*!

The ten most important pitfalls
1. **Fear of failure.** When making mistakes is painful and not generally accepted, this greatly impairs the learning process. Getting better is difficult when you're trying to avoid mistakes at all costs.

2. **Not being able to deal with transparency and openness.** To be able to work together and manage expectations, Scrum makes everything transparent: Backlogs, Burn-downs, Impediments, Daily Scrums, and Issues. In environments where people dislike transparency and openness, people don't like Scrum.

3. **Experiencing the problems that are exposed as too painful.** Because of the short iterations, you'll encounter new problems and imperfections every Sprint. This isn't always fun. It brings these things to the surface, but doesn't resolve them. Some environments cannot deal with this. So, not resolving problems when they appear and considering fighting symptoms as fighting the problems themselves is a potential pitfall.

4. **Managing Scrum teams in a controlling fashion.** Scrum teams should plan, estimate, look for improvements, and take responsibility for their results. This implies you should not try to manage Scrum teams by command and control, but based on goals and results. This requires a facilitating management style. If you don't do this, you'll fail.

5. **Deciding on details that the Scrum teams should decide on.** Decisions on details are the responsibility of the Scrum teams. Together with stakeholders, Scrum teams should make decisions. Managers should not intervene in this.

If you do intervene, Scrum teams will stop making decisions for themselves in the future.

6. **Not measuring the costs and returns of Scrum.** Adopting a new way of working costs time and money. Adopting Scrum is an investment. Investments should have positive returns. Sooner or later someone's going to ask what the costs and returns are. You should be able to answer such questions, so you should measure the costs and returns.

7. **Only measuring how happy everyone is.** An important aspect of Scrum is that it quickly energizes employees and customers. However, that's not a business case in itself. If the only proof you have available that Scrum is successful is that everyone's happy, you've come across another pitfall. Only talking about happy people isn't sufficient long term.

8. **Adapting Scrum before having even started.** An important pitfall to avoid is only taking aboard the "easy and painless" aspects of Scrum, so taking the revolution out of Scrum and adapting the current way of working (which has proven to be ineffective) a little, to make it look like Scrum. Without pain, there can never be true change.

9. **Only applying half of the Scrum practices while still calling the process Scrum.** Scrum isn't huge. Nevertheless, all aspects have a function. There's no "halfsies" in Scrum. If you try to do this anyway, you'll only end up "shooting yourself in the foot". The different aspects of Scrum are close-fitting and strengthen one another. Do as you wish, but Scrum is only Scrum if you do it for real. Period.

10. **Not measuring to what degree you're following Scrum.** As long as you don't make transparent how well Scrum's being

applied in your organization, everyone's free to say whatever they want. So, make a dashboard and make sure it's clear what you're doing and what you're not doing. Only then are you able to explain why certain things don't work and only then it's transparent how well things are really going.

Is combining Scrum and fixed-price contracts a pitfall?

A common standpoint is that Scrum and fixed-price contracts don't mix. This is based on the fact that Scrum allows expanding the scope based on new insights. The popular opinion is that this would make it impossible to stick to fixed-price contracts and that this is a large and common pitfall.

However, the opposite is true. Scrum is especially suited for fixed-price contracts. This is because the method by definition requires the budget and turnaround time to be fixed. Every Sprint has a fixed duration with fixed costs. Therefore, a fixed-price contract with a fixed end date is perfectly suited to be divided into a number of Sprints, each with a working end result.

Agreeing to a fixed set of requirements in a fixed-price contract is also possible with Scrum. This is always a difficult thing to do, but this isn't because of the followed methodology. As long as the scope isn't changed, the project will be delivered according to that scope. This is also true when using Scrum. However, in practice this isn't likely to play out like this. We know in advance that new insights will arise when you show working and tested results, which will result in the scope being re-opened for discussion. So, start by working together with the customer to build trust and show you're able to deliver working results in a predictable fashion. When this is achieved, discussing change of the scope will come more natural if necessary.

The tactic used by Scrum with respect to fixed-price/date/scope projects is that the project is divided in a large number of partial deliveries of working results. This prevents all the feedback being given at the very end. It's in the final phase that most regular projects incur the largest delays.

Therefore, adjustments in Scrum are done during the project, when it's still possible to do so. This brings additional benefits to the customer. Because the result brings value straight from the first Sprint, the payback time of the project is reduced considerably. Another option the customer has is stopping the project sooner because the result is sufficiently valuable.

What to do when it's impossible to subdivide the work?
We often meet teams or organizations that insist short Sprints are impossible. A multitude of reasons come up when we ask them why: the customer isn't up to it, testing takes too long, users are unwilling to contribute, we cannot finish anything in just two weeks, and so on.

Nevertheless, this isn't true. It's always possible to do short Sprints. It's always possible to divide work in small enough lumps to make it fit. If you're unable to do that, it's far too risky to even begin working at all. This is the core reason why work takes longer than anticipated. A one-hour job can take half an hour more or less than one hour. A three-month job is never completed in half the time but will frequently take four months. If you cannot subdivide bulky work items into smaller ones, first find out how to do that properly. You cannot start working on something you don't sufficiently comprehend to do. Doing so is the main cause of unpredictability of work.

The second reason is even more truthful: A customer pays for a working product. A Scrum team working with two-week Sprints will on average cost about $50.000 per Sprint. When a customer spends that kind of money, it makes sense that he or she expects to see a working product by the end of the Sprint. Moreover, the customer expects the value of this result to exceed $50.000!

It's just unacceptable for a team to not deliver a working product within a month. If you are currently in an environment where this is difficult or nigh impossible, you should resolve it as soon as possible for you have discovered a huge inefficiency in your organization. If you're unable to convert expenditures of that size into value, you're sailing a leaky boat! You should fix the leak in the boat as soon as possible. By starting to work in short Sprints, you'll soon discover the location of the leak and invent ways to (piece by piece) mend the damage.

In essence, all reasons that are uttered for claiming short two- to four-week Sprints cannot work are equally valid for processes using long cycles of months and months. So, in environments where these long cycles are used, problems with finishing on schedule and achieving sufficient quality are very common. The way to turn this around is by starting to work with short one-week Sprints. Doing so forces making things small and manageable and avoids leaving unresolved issues. Paradoxically, introducing short Sprints is especially powerful in situations and environments where they seem the least likely to be feasible at all. Try it!

So there's only one response when people claim they cannot subdivide a piece of work: just do it!

What should you avoid doing?

- Considering mistakes and failure as bad things.
- Not acting to address things you painfully learn should improve.
- Thinking that because something seems or is difficult you shouldn't do it.
- Being afraid to make mistakes or punishing someone for making mistakes.
- Hiding mistakes so no-one's able to learn from them.
- Using transparency and openness against someone.
- Managing Scrum teams in a controlling fashion.
- Deciding on details that the Scrum teams should decide on.
- Not measuring the costs and returns of Scrum because it seems too difficult.
- Only measuring how happy everyone is.
- Only applying half of the Scrum practices while still calling it Scrum.
- Adapting Scrum before having even started.
- Thinking and communicating that Scrum and fixed-price contracts don't mix.
- Accepting the argument that a big chunk of work really can't be worked out in more detail.
- Starting to work on something that's too big to be able to make a working result in one Sprint.

HOW TO BUILD SCRUM TEAMS?

ALLOW TEAMS TO CREATE THEMSELVES UNDER THE CONDITION THAT THEY'LL DELIVER WORKING RESULTS IN ONE SPRINT

— CHAPTER 9 —

HOW TO BUILD SCRUM TEAMS?

An important task of a manager used to be dividing his people's time across the various projects. This is often a complex puzzle because usually there are often too many projects and too few people.

With Scrum, this changes. In Scrum, there are stable cross-functional teams. This means that Scrum teams consist of people with all the necessary skills to transform an idea of the Product Owner into a working result in one Sprint. Such a team chooses the duration of a Sprint. The rule of thumb is, the more dynamic the team needs to be, the shorter the Sprints need to be. The situation you want to be in is one where unexpected events don't disrupt the running Sprint but are included in the next Sprint with the help of the Product Owner. This makes a good Product Owner who includes all stakeholders and has sufficient authority to make decisions essential to allow Scrum teams to be successful. If such a Product Owner is present, changes will follow the normal Scrum rhythm.

The best way to create Scrum teams is by allowing them to construct and organize themselves. It's best that Scrum teams work towards realizing business goals directly.

And just to make sure: Scrum teams do not have a project leader! Leading, coordinating, and organizing are done by the team itself, as a joint effort by all the team members.

"Do you have a minute? I'm working on dividing my people into Scrum teams and I feel like I'm not doing it right."

"Oh, why?"

"Well, I divide people with similar knowledge across teams while I'd feel more comfortable putting them together. If I'd put them together then I can at least be sure they'll share their knowledge and I won't be dependent on a particular individual. What it the only guy that knows Java in a team gets sick? Will the rest of the team be stuck waiting for him to get better?"

"I get what you mean. You want to combine comparable skills in one team so the team members are able to cover for each other when necessary."

"Exactly! I'm not so sure about those cross-functional teams. I think the damage to knowledge expansion is much bigger than any benefits. Further teams become much more vulnerable."

"I understand where you're coming from, but you're wrong anyway. Let me ask you this: What university in the Netherlands offers a degree in Java development or T-map testing?"

"What do you mean?"

"Exactly what I say. Where are your people trained to be specialists? What school teaches them that?"

"Well, none of course. They're trained to be computer scientists or mathematicians or something."

"Exactly! We turn them into specialists, but they aren't specialists by nature. I hope you see that you're creating problems for yourself by trying to put people with similar skills into a single team. By dividing the competencies across the teams the people in the teams are able to learn from each other and expand their skills. After a while, you won't have just one Java team but ten teams with knowledge of Java. This will make you much more agile. It's also more enjoyable for your people. Doing new things and doing varying work is much more fun than creating as much Java code as possible with eight guys, only to hand it over to the team of testers. So make teams that are able to win the game together. This is much more energizing!"

"But how do you make sure you retain specialist skills? How do you prevent ending up with a bunch of generalists?"

"Simple answer: by buying pizzas. Specialists will seek each other out, no matter what you do. They want to improve in their specialty and actively want to learn. They'll organize this themselves. An ideal way to do this is in guilds."

"Okay, just like the football team of my son: they have a specific striker training."

"Yes exactly, and if you don't provide this for them, they'll arrange it themselves. Many strikers stay after the training to work on their finishing. Improving is an intrinsic motivation."

"Well, maybe you're right."

"Why don't you just try it and see if it works? If it doesn't, you can still change it after a few months. A final tip though: allow your people to build their own teams. They'll be able to do this much faster! But maybe we should talk about that some more another time."

"Yes, let's do that. You've given me plenty to think about for now."

The five things that need to be taken care of before you start a Scrum team

1. **An empowered Product Owner.** Get a Product Owner who has sufficient power to make decisions and at least 50% of his time available to dedicate to the role of Product Owner. Sufficient decision-making powers means the Product Owner can make decisions about the work in at least the next three Sprints for himself. At the start, being a Product Owner should be his primary task; this is why we ask at least 50% of his time. The first goal of the Product Owner is composing an ordered Product Backlog and, as such, to optimize the value the team can deliver. A good Product Owner includes stakeholders and organizes workshops to involve them in making decisions. Don't forget the base rule: A Scrum team only has one Product Owner and only works on one Product Backlog.

2. **A stable and strong Development Team.** Scrum works because of stable full-time teams that get the opportunity to get well-attuned and improve. Therefore, the makeup of the team should be clear before the team starts. Very few things are more detrimental than changes in the makeup of the team in the first few Sprints. Make the teams sufficiently large so they're able to absorb small internal disturbances. In practice, this usually means teams of five through seven people. Furthermore, make sure there is sufficient "rowing power" in the Development Team. With rowing power we mean team members who actually make, design, or test things.

3. **A team space with supporting materials.** It's important to have access to a calm working environment with sufficient wall space for hanging the Product Backlog and Scrum boards. Also arrange for sufficient computers, chairs, tables,

Scrum boards, post-its, markers, etc. All this seems obvious but in practice we run into all sort of weird things. Team spaces without tables and chairs are no exception. We've also encountered teams that needed to wait a month for their computers to arrive. Finally we've seen it can take up to three months to order a whiteboard.

4. **A Scrum Master.** It's very important to have a Scrum Master who helps the team to get better. Therefore, it makes sense to work with full-time Scrum Masters who are dedicated to that role. Avoid part-time Scrum Masters that are also members of the Development Team. It's usually not effective. This is especially important in the beginning when the team still has a lot to learn and the people outside of the Scrum team are still unsure how best to help a Scrum team.

5. **Active monitoring and guidance.** Make sure it's clear for everyone how the progress will be measured. This should be done on the dashboard and with the reports from the transition roadmap. Make transparent the degree in which the Development Team, Scrum Master, and Product Owner are able to carry out their roles. Also make sure there's a Scrum coach available who has time to help the Scrum team in the first few Sprints.

How is the Sprint length of a team decided?

How long a Scrum takes should be based on how dynamic the situation is. Is there a lot of change? Then choose to work using short Sprints. Are there many incidents and disturbances? Then also opt for shorts Sprints. Also do this when frequent changes in direction are needed, the Scrum team is inexperienced, or the environment is very complex.

With complex systems, you should only make small changes. This is because everything's interconnected. You shouldn't try to change twenty things before you check the result because anything unexpected might be caused by one of the twenty changes *or* some interaction between these changes. If something is complex, you should change one thing at a time and immediately check the result. If something goes wrong, then you immediately know the cause. In short, the more dynamic the situation the shorter the Sprints.

The most common Sprint length in practice is two weeks. This is long enough to create added value and short enough to remain visible and be able to change direction. Furthermore, we generally see that teams that use four-week Sprints create the same value in those four weeks as teams using two-week Sprints create in two weeks. So you can choose: do you want 13 value increments a year or 26? The choice seems straightforward.

When starting out with Scrum it's a good idea to use one-week Sprints. This is because the team's still unfamiliar with Scrum and with a one-week Sprint they go through the Scrum rhythm 52 times a year. This helps in picking up Scrum faster. After about three months it's usually the right moment to discuss what "definitive" Scrum length you choose to use. When the team's able to work predictably in one-week Sprints, it's fine to make the Sprints longer. If the team can't yet do this, definitely don't make the Sprints longer just yet. This means the team isn't yet able to organize itself in an attainable and realistic fashion. Make sure you solve this issue first. Giving the team more time by expanding the Sprint length isn't the solution. That's just avoiding the problem.

In short, choose the Sprint length in such a way that when something unexpected occurs, this can flow to the team via the Product Backlog. If the occurrence of an unexpected event makes it necessary to disturb the current Sprint of the team, this means the Sprint length is too long. The Sprint rhythm is an approach to being flexible. The shorter the Sprints the higher the flexibility.

With multiple Scrum teams it's a good idea to align the chosen Sprint lengths. This is practical when Team 1 depends on Team 2 for something or when you still deliver to the market at one specific time.

By aligning the Sprint length you create a steady rhythm throughout the company.

Who to put in which Scrum team?

What's the best way to divide your people into Scrum teams? This is quite a difficult puzzle. In fact, it's a complex problem. Especially when people are involved, the total number of combinations may seem near infinite. How do you solve this?

Well, with two steps. Step one is about determining what the teams should adhere to. Step two is allowing the teams to construct themselves.

Self-organizing should start on the first day. Why should you as manager be better able to divide the people into teams than the people themselves are? All these people combined have more brains than you alone, so their combined intellect is higher than yours. But they should make the division within certain boundaries. Deciding what those boundaries or constraints are is your job. What type of boundaries are we talking about? Well, you decide how many people form a team. The optimum Scrum team size is three to nine members. Team size should be chosen so that the teams will be able to absorb small disturbances within the team (e.g., a sick day or dentist appointment), while having all the necessary skills to create the product increment (working result). In practice, this means that Scrum teams usually have between five and seven members. Never encourage teams of more than nine people. In such teams the communication overhead is way too big. Two teams with five team members are much more effective than one team with ten members.

Another requirement you prescribe is the competences and seniority in the team. For example, you could say you want a mix of experience and junior people, like at least 30% of each. With respect to competences, you should demand that each team turn the idea of a Product Owner into a working result in a single Sprint. Note that we're talking about competences and not roles. Everyone's role is team member; an example of a competence is marketing and communication. It's easy to compare it to a soccer team: goalkeeping is a competence but when the goalkeeper is sick you won't play without a goalkeeper. If necessary the striker will put on gloves and protect the net; it's an essential competence to play a game.

You can also specify additional restrictions, such as discouraging making teams of friends. Ask people with friends in the company to not join the same team. Also explain why you ask them this. Putting them in the same team would be a missed opportunity for the company because they'll be the glue between teams when they're part of different teams. Also explain that a team for resolving incidents is not allowed: each team is responsible for solving its own incidents to make delivering quality intrinsic.

Also make sure the people understand that only complete teams are allowed. So don't allow half teams such as a team with testers but no design competencies or a "rest-team" of people that are left. Furthermore, ask teams to come up with a team name for their team, make a logo and decorate their own team space. All this is aimed at making the team a real team. This pays off and is also fair as they'll be collaborating intensively for a long period.

The final and maybe most important restriction is that everyone should agree with the proposal for the division into teams. Some people will have to make sacrifices for the greater good, but this should be their own decision. Everybody should have the right to veto the proposal. Being assigned to a team against your will undermines the entire concept of a self-organizing team. You cannot accept the situation in which people complain they were forced into this. You should explicitly ask: "Does everyone agree? Is this unanimous? This is the moment to speak up if you don't agree". Feel free to add that this is only a starting division and that making changes to this later is possible. Of course those changes should adhere to the boundaries you decided on!

Does a Scrum team really not have a project manager?

In Scrum there is no project leader or project manager.

In Scrum leading the project is divided among three roles. The *what* and *why* is the responsibility of the Product Owner, the *how* is the responsibility of the Development Team, and the *framework* and making sure this continuously *improves* is the responsibility of the Scrum Master.

In practice, we often see that in the transition to Scrum, those that used to be project managers become Scrum Masters and the teams stay the same. This can work, but usually this makes it difficult for the team members to really take on their new ways of working. In their perception little has changed compared to the old situation. Sometimes project managers also become the assistants of Product Owners.

We advise to strictly adhere to the role Scrum prescribes. If you do decide to deviate from this, make sure it's clear who's responsible for what. If possible, discontinue the role of project leader or project manager and put all the work within the team. Removing the project leader and project manager functions as official functions in the company can be a very good intervention to really change things.

We realize this is not possible in some environments. Do take care, however, that the teams are expected to take on their new responsibilities even though there's still a project leader present.

In large-scale programs or complex projects with multiple Scrum teams and systems, we often see the role of project leader is recreated. This is often the right thing to do. Such situations are discussed in Chapter 13. For now it's sufficient to say that Scrum doesn't have a project leader role but that these responsibilities are divided over the Product Owner, Scrum Master, and the Development Team.

This is because leading and managing is so important we cannot trust the project leader to do this on his or her own!

How to do personnel management for Scrum teams?

The Scrum team takes care of its own operational personnel management. The manager just defines the boundaries for this. Effectiveness is the keyword in this. You want everyone to be working to the best of his or her ability while being motivated and energetic to best help the company. Self-improvement and putting first the customer and the best interests of the company are part of this.

In traditional companies this happens on an individual basis. The senior judges his or her subordinates and is, in turn, judged by his or her boss, and so on. For actually doing the work, we assign the people (in some extreme cases even called resources) to the work and judge their contributions.

Scrum turns this process around by working in stable teams. Now the team as a whole should be judged and the judging of individual team members is only done inside the team itself. That's it. Of course you should provide the teams with the boundaries in which they should do this. Allow the teams to do as much as they can themselves and help the trams when needed.

A useful tool to help teams to look at themselves is the model provided by the book *The Five Dysfunctions of a Team* by Patrick Lencioni. You can use this model to help teams look in the mirror. We have encountered teams who like to use the model every couple of months in their Sprint Retrospectives. How well do we really function as a team?

For teams to achieve goal-driven and guaranteed results it's necessary they take responsibility, commit themselves, sometimes fight and trust each other. Usually, it does take a while for all this to materialize. As a manager, you should play an important role in this. The faster you can help a group of people to become a solid team, the faster you'll see better results.

Appraising individuals still exists. There will always be over-performers and under-performers. As a manager, you should be able to act on that. You should help over-performers to grow and help underperformers in becoming better or cut them loose. To do this, you need input from the team. In the end, the team result is all that matters. But this is achieved through individual contributions.

What should you do?

- Appoint a good Product Owner with the power to make decisions.
- Define the right boundaries for a stable and strong Development Team.
- Facilitate a Team Space with accessories.
- Appoint an experienced Scrum Master for coaching the team.
- Facilitate active monitoring and guidance.
- Determine the Scrum length based on how dynamic the situation is.
- Choose short one-week Sprints if the situation is very dynamic.
- Determine requirements for Scrum teams to fulfil.
- Allow people to construct their own Scrum teams.
- Allow Scrum teams to lead themselves: do not appoint a project leader.
- Teach Scrum teams to do their own operational personnel management.
- Guide individual team members to make the team better.

HOW TO MONITOR SCOPE AND PROGRESS IN SCRUM?

THERE'S ONLY ONE METRIC FOR MEASURING PROGRESS: THE DELIVERED VALUE OF THE WORKING AND TESTED RESULT!

— CHAPTER 10 —

HOW TO MONITOR SCOPE AND PROGRESS IN SCRUM?

The essence of Scrum is continuously giving priority to the most valuable thing and really finishing it. If you're only halfway done with something, it doesn't have any value. Don't feel satisfied because you've completed a certain percentage of some task. Make it truly simple for yourself: it's either done or it isn't.

This should also be what you tell your people as a manager: whether something's done is the only thing that counts. This means you should focus on that. So, you should be present at all Sprint Reviews as this is where the finished products are shown. It also means you should keep track of the Burn-up and Burn-down charts across Sprints. Those are the artifacts that show what is finished. You don't have to maintain these overview charts yourself. All progress is already measured and visualized by the Scrum team itself.

The only thing you have to do is show that you only use transparent backlogs, visual progress, and Burn-down and Burn-up charts to measure progress and nothing else. In the end, there's only one metric for measuring progress: the value of the result that's finished already. So this is also the way to monitor the scope. If this is going how it should be, nothing else truly matters.

So steer towards valuable results!

"I want to get rid of those story points. I want to go back to using hours! The story points are meaningless to me: I have no idea when something's going to be done. I was able to do that with hours, so let's get back to using those!"

"Wait a minute, I think you're confusing two things. Making sure you realize a forecast and coming up with that forecast are two completely different things. If you're constantly showing you're unable to realize forecasts, then how much do those forecasts say about the future to begin with?"

"Nothing at all!"

"Exactly. This is why we first try to teach Scrum team to be able to realize their forecasts. This is usually difficult when using hours."

"Oh, why?"

"Well, because people in general are bad at estimating how many hours something will take. We're generally way too optimistic. It's very common for us to take two days to finish an amount of work we estimated at eight hours. Something we estimate at eight hours takes sixteen. This may seem contradictory, but it's true. Do you recognize this?"

"Yes, I actually do. I'm often amazed at how little I really achieve in a day. A meeting of an hour usually takes me more than an hour. If I include preparation and the meeting taking longer, I regularly spend two hours."

"Precisely, so you're already using a point scale for making estimates. Instead of forecasting hours, you forecast the number of meetings. Apparently four meetings a day is your pace. That's exactly how Scrum teams do it. This helps them in becoming predictable, which will help them make more accurate forecasts."

"But why can't they do that by forecasting how many hours it will take?"

"Just look at yourself. If you have four meetings on a day that would be a total of four hours, right? If you'd have estimated in hours you would have thought you still have half a day available for other things."

"Yeah, but I don't."

"Exactly. This is also how the teams do it. Based on past experience they know how many points the can process in a week and this helps them in becoming predictable. Do you get that?"

"Yes, I do. What I still don't understand though is how I can tell when something's going to be finished. I have to know this to be able to make commitments."

"You know what I'll do?"

"Well?"

"I'll plan a regular meeting with all the Product Owners. We'll commit to making a weekly graph showing the overall progress. Nothing complicated. The graph will have two lines. The first line shows the amount of work that's on the Backlog and the second will show how much work the teams have finished. This will help you in making realistic forecasts and commitments."

"Sounds good! Excellent proposal. I'm going to take immediate action for this."

"You're what?"

"Well, I'm cancelling a meeting. I have a daily limit of four meetings, remember?"

Measuring progress with results

Scrum offers something valuable which isn't always recognized. With Scrum, you're able to steer based on results. Because most of what we do involves non-tangible things, we've taught ourselves to steer using the process. This makes everything much more complex than it needs to be, because the connection between process and result isn't always predictable. Next to this, the process also consists of many parameters. An alternative is steering on the result.

To be able to do this, the system needs to change. This is exactly what Jeff Sutherland and Ken Schwaber have done when they designed Scrum. They totally changed the rules of the game. By working in short cycles which each deliver a working result, steering based on that result is possible!

A secondary effect is that many popular process indicators were used to measure meticulously have become obsolete. Just look at the number of worked hours. This isn't a very good indicator of progress, is it? If I've been cooking for three hours, how much does that really tell you about how close I am to finishing the meal? Not very much, right? By lack of anything better, many organizations have taken up measuring the number of hours spent on something as a measure for progress and as the basis for forecasts.

With Scrum, you don't forecast in hours but in finished results. This is much better since this metric is much closer to what you're actually delivering to the customer. Worked hours aren't even important anymore for measuring costs since the costs of Sprints are constant. Stable teams result in stable costs per Sprint. So hours are a bad way to measure costs; counting the number of Sprints is much better. This brings charging the customer per successfully completed Sprint within arm's reach.

Monitoring progress and scope with a Burn-up chart

A good way to measure progress across Sprints is with a Burn-up chart. This is a line graph that summarizes across Sprints how much work a Scrum team (or collection of Scrum teams) has completed.

The first line in the graph is a line depicting the amount of work that needs to be delivered to the customer. This consists of all the work on the Product Backlog up until the first time you want to deliver the work to the customer. The second line in the graph shows the number of completed story points. We add these together for every Sprint, so in the graph you'll see the second line slowly approaching the first line. If you add extra work to the goal, you'll see a rise in the goal line as well. Conversely, if you remove work from your goal, you'll see top line dropping as well. When the two lines touch, you've reached your goal and can deliver the product to your customer.

An important way to steer is by managing scope. This is done by the Product Owner using the Product Backlog. Scrum teams should complete everything they do every Sprint; so, by reducing the scope, you'll be able to deliver to your customer sooner. It's always possible to expand the scope again at a later time. This makes time your friend, as opposed to your enemy. Drawing trend lines allow you to be predictable. Draw a positive and negative trend line along the actual results. By looking at these lines, you'll be perfectly able to forecast when everything will be done.

The Product Owner maintains this Burn-up chart between Sprints. This will take very little time and help make it easier to determine whether expectations are realistic or not. The Product Owner should hang this graph next to the Product Backlog. That way, everyone that walks by will be able to easily see the current status.

It's crucial you don't "punish" teams for delivering less results or failing to finish a Sprint in time. Instead, help them become more predictable in the future. This is the only way for organizations to become predictable as a whole. Focus on a small set of the most valuable things and complete this. It's always possible to expand the Scope later.

In short, monitor scope and progress by concrete results and steer using the Product Backlog. The Product Owner should take the lead in this. As manager, you're able to speed up the teams by removing impediments.

Four additional devices for measuring progress

The Burn-up chart is an important device for measuring progress and making this transparent. It's surprising how few Scrum teams and Product Owners make use of this chart. Consequently, Scrum teams are shrouded in fog because it's unclear what their current status is. Transparency is extremely important. The Burn-up chart is ideal for being transparent. Next to it, there are four more devices for measuring progress.

1. **The Scrum board.** Scrum teams maintain their own Scrum board (showing the Sprint Backlog) during the Sprint. All tasks of the current Sprint flow from To Do, via In Progress, to Done. This makes the Scrum board an excellent way to visualize and measure progress within a Sprint for the Development Team.

2. **The Daily Scrum.** Additionally, everyone's allowed to attend the Daily Scrum. By attending a Daily Scrum as a listener (only the Development Team speak), you immediately know the current status of the team. And it only takes fifteen minutes.

3. **The Burn-down chart.** A device for determining whether the work for the current Sprint is still attainable within that Sprint is the Burn-down chart. This is practical because the number of tasks on the Scrum board can be quite daunting, making it difficult to get an overview. Most teams create a Burn-down chart and put this on the wall next to the Scrum board. The Burn-down chart depicts the amount of work done in the current Sprint and, therefore, indicates whether the team is running behind schedule or not. If the amount of completed work is below the trend line, the team is behind schedule. If the amount of completed work is above the trend line, the team is ahead of schedule.

4. **The Sprint Review.** Finally, the Sprint Review is the ideal time to track progress. This is where the teams show their working results.

What's the scope if you can constantly change it?

A common complaint is that you don't know what you end up with when you work with Scrum. You'll get a present at the end, but it's a surprise what it'll be! The easiest way to counter this complaint is by saying that this is also true for fully planned processes with long cycles. Just look at the results: results are often late, end up costing too much, and are of inferior quality. All a meticulously worked out plan offers is a false sense of security about what you'll end up with. Before you start, you already know that not everything will go according to plan.

With Scrum, you also need a vision of where you're heading: a dot on the horizon. However, you don't need to make a long detailed document for this. Having a rough sketch is enough. Scrum teams need to know what they're working towards. Call it the product vision or roadmap or just call it the Product Backlog. When looking to the future without a Backlog it's difficult to forecast or estimate.

It's striking that many organizations that used to plan years in advance in a very detailed fashion switch to Scrum and then suddenly think you don't ever need to look ahead more than two weeks. They go from one extreme to the other. Having a view of where you're going is important with Scrum as well. This is the reason of the emphasis on doing workshops with customers, end users, and other stakeholders to jointly construct a Product Backlog that looks far into the future.

The big advantage of Scrum is that the whole Backlog doesn't need to be worked out in great detail. It's better if you don't divide the backlog into features but into themes or epics. An example is the theme "doubling the ability to plan work". How exactly you're going to realize this theme is decided at a later time. You only know that, whatever's going to be done for this theme, it should double the ability to plan work to be successful.

So you should describe the scope in the value it provides to the customer. Don't work out what the exact outcome will be, but what you're trying to achieve with it. In the end, that's all that matters. This does require you to look at things from the viewpoint of customer value rather than functional properties. This can be tricky at the start before everyone gets how to properly do this.

Six measures for fixed-price Scrum

The flexibility provided by a series of Sprints with working results makes it possible to manage projects with a fixed price, date, or scope with Scrum. By always giving priority to the highest added value and by continuously delivering a working system, it's possible to commit to creating the maximum attainable value within the available time and budget. You should do this using the following six measures:

1. **Use customer value for guidance.** Don't focus on functionality but rather on customer value. When you do this, it's not necessary to work out the needed functionality in detail in advance. This can be done later. Just commit to solving the underlying issue to the best of your ability. This saves a lot of time building detailed specifications that aren't needed and only provide limited value.

2. **Compose user stories and order them on value.** User stories describe functionality from the perspective of the user and from the perspective of creating value. By ordering these user stories based on their value, it's possible to start with the most valuable ones. This enables you to create the most value, each and every Sprint.

3. **Use "exchange requests" instead of change requests.** "Exchange requests" are change requests in which you also indicate at the expense of what this change should be done. In other words, if you add more work, something of the same

size should be dropped as well. By doing this, the scope will stay frozen while becoming more accurate at the same time. Doing this requires the customer to "get" Scrum.

4. **Reserve a budget for contingencies.** Also with Scrum it's advisable to reserve time in a fixed-price/date/scope project that isn't in advance assigned to anything. This can be used do unforeseen work or make extra functionality. Furthermore, this budget allows you to give the customer a "present" once in a while.

5. **Have customers approve intermediate results.** The Sprint Review is an ideal time to get feedback on, and approval of, the work you've done so far. Don't postpone the approval to the very last Sprint. Have the customer approve everything you deliver (assuming it's something that really works). By doing this, you continuously test each other's understanding.

6. **Offer the possibility to stop sooner.** Because you deliver a working result every Sprint, you have the option of stopping whenever this working result is "good enough". Therefore, it's interesting to explain to the customer this is possible. This makes the business case even stronger. In a fixed-price contract, you can agree that if the customer decides to stop sooner, he or she still needs to pay part of the agreed price in the contract.

What should you avoid doing?

- Steer based on finished products, preferably through a Burn-up chart that you put on the wall.
- Make sure that you work based on a vision and worked out Product Backlog.
- Make sure the Product Backlog emphasizes delivering value instead of specifying the concrete work.
- Regularly inspect the Scrum board of the teams (without saying a word).
- Incidentally attend the Daily Scrum (without saying a word).
- Inspect the Burn-down chart of the team (without saying a word).
- Give feedback in the Sprint Review meeting (and make sure you seldom miss it).
- Only work with fixed-price-Scrum when the customer "gets" Scrum.
- Measure progress through outcomes instead of output.

HOW TO BE PREDICTABLE AND PRODUCTIVE WITH SCRUM?

COLLECT METRICS, FOCUS ON GETTING BETTER, AND ONLY MAKE COMMITMENTS IN TERMS OF CUSTOMER VALUE

— CHAPTER 11 —

HOW TO BE PREDICTABLE AND PRODUCTIVE WITH SCRUM?

Working iteratively and creating a working result every Sprint helps make you more predictable. It won't be a surprise at the end if something doesn't work. Every Sprint you'll see progress and your view of what is attainable and what isn't will improve. Revising forecasts isn't a bad thing, as long as you do it early enough. Only indicating at the very last moment something isn't going to work can have dramatic consequences. So, measure progress and make this transparent by maintaining a Burn-up chart and drawing trend lines.

Be sure to also discuss these charts with customers and other stakeholders. They can help by adapting the scope or removing impediments. It's also crucial to stop making concrete plans. Try to only make commitments regarding the value you'll deliver and the problems you'll solve and not about what functionality will be there. Along the way, you should be able to adapt your plan based on new insights.

Solving the problem in another way should always be a valid option. You don't want a successful operation with a dead patient but a cured patient, even though you replaced the operation with a therapy.

In the end, it's about the complete result, not how you got there.

"Hey, don't your teams work according to Scrum? Doesn't that mean they don't need to specify everything to you in detail?"

"Yes, you're right."

"Good, since we're looking for a way to see how our customers use social media and use this to increase our sales. How many Sprints will that take? What will it cost?"

"Pfff, no idea."

"What kind of answer is that? I want to know what it'll cost!"

"Yes, I get that, but if all you can tell me is that it's something to do with social media, I won't be able to tell you what it'll cost. But, let's talk about what I can do."

"Okay, good idea. What can you do?"

"What you could do is give me an indication how much you're willing to spend. What do you expect this project will make you? So what are you willing to spend? Any idea?"

"Pfff, that's a tough question. That really depends on whether keeping an eye on the use of social media by our customers will land us any sales at all. We expect this, but aren't sure."

"Okay, clear. What are you willing to spend to find out whether this idea can make money?"

"Well, let's see. If we're able to land one extra sale it would already be interesting and I wouldn't need to profit on that. Say $50,000, but it can be slightly more or less."

"Okay, got it. I can work with that. We have four Scrum teams working for you right now. Let's ask one of those teams to spend half of their time on this for a month. This will cost 50k. This team will transform your idea into a working result in four Sprints and you'll be able to use this working result to monitor the social media activity of your customers. Don't expect it to be perfect, but it'll support the most important things."

"Okay, you could stick with Twitter for now and restrict it for those customers whose Twitter usernames we know. If we do that we should be able to see whether it works quickly."

"Yes, that's an option, but maybe there are better options. Attend the refinement session. You know, the workshops of about an hour in which we work on the Product Backlog?"

"Yes, I do. Aren't they always from four to five in the afternoon?"

"Exactly. Be sure to attend these. In those meetings the team decides what to do first. Then we'll be able to quickly find out whether it works."

"Good idea! If it makes us as much as we think, I'll be able to secure more funding."

"I get that. Let's start by showing it indeed works and see how much extra sales it generates. Then you can immediately use what we have built to make money."

"Perfect!"

What kind of commitments help with being more predictable?

Working with Scrum gives you opportunities. Because you change the rigid scope to a flexible one and you finish everything you do, you can make different kinds of commitments. For example, you can commit to always finishing on time. This is easy to commit to because the result is always finished at the end of every Sprint. You know the number of Sprints before a certain date and you always deliver the highest attainable value.

You can also commit to delivering a constant quality level (usually higher than before) because you test and deliver much more frequently. In the end, you'll have a constant transparent quality level and the customer knows exactly what will be delivered.

Further, you can commit to always being transparent and honest. You show all progress in Burn-up and Burn-down charts, the Scrum board is on the wall, as is the Product Backlog and following each and every Sprint, you demonstrate the working and tested results.

Next to this, you can also commit to never asking detailed questions for decisions that are still a long way off. You'll determine that together with the customer when it matters. Until that time, it's not necessary to go over hypothetical "what-if" scenarios. We'll focus on those when they materialize.

A final important commitment you're able to make is the ability to advance things. You're able to advance what's most important to the front of the queue and deliver it first. This is completely different from what many customers are used to. Reason from the perspective of the customer and advance what's important. You can commit to being open for early adjustments. You don't need to rigidly stick to a plan that no longer applies. You're able to move around when this is appropriate.

All this makes real collaboration attainable.

Why do we express our estimates in points instead of hours?

It's best to measure progress in working results. It's only possible to be predictable when you deliver on the agreed times. Therefore, a metric based on finished results is superior to a metric based on the number of worked hours. So, try to switch from estimating and tracking progress in hours to story points as soon as possible. Story points are awarded on a relative scale for finished results.

In general, people are very bad at estimating how long something will take. This is because time expressed in hours is an absolute unit and people are bad at estimating absolute units. On the other hand, people are very good at estimating relatively. If we see a tower, we find it very difficult to estimate its height. However, when two towers stand next to each other, we can tell in a second that the second tower is twice as high as the first. Another disadvantage of estimating in hours is that it's very tempting to use them in misleading calculations. Two people aren't guaranteed to finish sixteen hours of work in a day just like nine women cannot reduce the pregnancy duration from nine months to one.

To measure and estimate, Scrum encourages a method that decouples the unit of relative size from the turnaround time. The points are an indication of the size of the result and the turnaround time is calculated by dividing the number of points by the number of points the team completes in a Sprint. Estimating is done by the entire Scrum team as a joint activity. The usual way to do this is with Planning Poker. Most teams use a scale in which the precision decreases as the size of the numbers increases (0, ½, 1, 2, 3, 5, 8, 13, 20, 40, 100, etc.).

For example, say we need to weigh some fruit. We assign a strawberry 1 point, an apple 5, and a watermelon 100 points. Using this scale, we can assign a value to all types of fruit. A grape is ½ point and a tangerine 3. Try it for yourself. Without knowing the exact weight of any type of fruit it's still easy to assign these relative numbers to all types of fruit.

This is also how it's done in Scrum teams. Deciding on what is meant with 1, 5, and 20 points and estimating all other tasks relative to that. How many points can be completed by a Scrum team in a Sprint is discovered by experience very quickly. Using this information, it becomes possible to make accurate predictions based on the trend lines on the Burn-up chart. This makes the results of a team predictable.

What if the people in your organization are used to estimating using hours? What if the reporting is done using estimated and worked hours? If you are able to change this, do so, but choose your battles wisely. An added bonus is that the number of story points a team completes each Sprint will increase over time. This makes running ahead of schedule and finishing earlier a possibility. Isn't that great?

How to realize a continuous increase in productivity?

The promise sounds amazing: continuously improving teams who increase their productivity to hyper-productivity, increasing twentyfold from what they were able to do before. But is this really possible? Isn't there a limit to how productive a team can become?

Of course everything has a limit. Professional athletes are all too aware of this. The world record for the marathon is little over two hours. This record is likely to be overthrown in the future, but it will never be under one hour. Somewhere between one hour and the current time lies the absolute limit of human ability. A similar limit must exist for team productivity, right?

This is partially true. At the same time, many organizations aren't even close to running into this limit. There is so much left to improve that talking about it isn't useful. We should first try to get anywhere close to the limit. Just like with the marathon. Everyone that truly wants to can run a Marathon in four hours. Just start training and improving.

Take note, getting better doesn't imply working harder. Many teams confuse the two. Working smarter: yes. Working harder: no. Working harder only wears you out. If you do this, peaks in productivity will be followed by valleys that are deeper than the peaks are high. So, try to work with in a stable maintainable pace, just like someone running a marathon. Help your teams in achieving this.

So, help to prevent too much work being assigned to a Sprint. Help the teams in taking on the most important thing and really finishing this.

The productivity of a Scrum team is mostly determined through the Product Backlog. The Product Backlog determines the outcome of a team just as much as their actual output. In other words, it's not important how a much a kilogram of a product costs; what matters is the impact of that kilogram. The biggest increase in productivity is achieved by what the team does, not by how they do it. Therefore, be sure to help the Product Owner in prioritizing the Product Backlog and communicating with customers.

The Product Backlog is the instrument to measure and help increase productivity. Of course, the Product Owner plays an important role in this. The good news is that as a manager, you can help the Product Owner. Make it a goal of the team to have a high rate of improvement instead of a high development speed, help by removing impediments, help by rigorously ordering the Backlog, and safeguard the team from being swamped with work.

Nine measures to further improve productivity

Striving for efficiency is undesirable. What matters is effectiveness. Efficiency in a chain leads to delays and usually a decrease in effectiveness. Flow is much more important. How long does it take for a question by the customer to be answered? How long does it take for a business opportunity to be converted to a working product? Effectiveness helps customers while efficiency is just fooling yourself.

But what can you do as a manager to increase the effectiveness of Scrum teams?

1. **Order the backlog.** In the end, the value of the input limits the potential value of the output. Upfront, many organizations only have a vague idea about the potential value of an idea. Help to make this concrete by filling the Product Backlog.

2. **Let teams make their own achievements transparent.** Help Scrum teams to become self-organizing and self-improving. Don't do this by actively checking what they do, but by asking them to make their results and achievements transparent and by allowing them to discover for themselves how to improve.

3. **Celebrate.** Good results deserve to be properly celebrated. Make sure this happens. Reward good results. Success is contagious so it will stimulate both the teams that are already successful and those that aren't yet because they see that success is appreciated. It's about attention, appreciation, and fun. Cake, champagne, flowers or a public pat on the back are excellent ways to do this.

4. **Help with removing impediments.** Many things that slow teams down are outside of their control. A manager can and should play an important role removing these impediments. Help to streamline the organization and processes to allow teams to perform better.

5. **Present yourself as a coach, mentor, and source of inspiration.** The only way for teams to truly become self-organizing is by allowing them to stand on their own feet. This means biting your tongue, not giving unsolicited advice, and asking a lot of questions. These should be open questions! The best questions start with "What", "How", and "Why".

6. **Help teams increase energy levels and morale.** Perhaps this sounds a bit soft, but experience has shown us that the morale of a team has an enormous influence on the results. If everyone is full of energy and motivation, teams are able to move mountains. Teams won't be able to do this by themselves. They have to learn to do this and need your help.

7. **Focus on flow.** In the end, the flow rate is what customers perceive. So measure this. Avoid that Scrum teams be clogged with work or clog themselves. The inclination to do more will only result in "traffic jams". If teams don't ask you about it, be sure to monitor their WIP limits (Work in progress limits). How much work can they handle before they're clogged?

8. **Make improvement and increase the rate of improvement goals and measure these.** In the end, the passing of time will resolve all issues if teams have a positive improvement rate. You can measure and monitor this rate. Even relatively slow teams with a large improvement rate will eventually overtake relatively fast teams.

9. **Emphasize that working harder is never an option and working smarter is.** Keep repeating this. You improve the outcome via the Product Backlog and the output by working smarter. Working harder doesn't work. Aim for a balance between sharpening the axe (improving) and chopping down trees (doing).

Devices to mutually compare Scrum teams

The usefulness of mutually comparing Scrum teams is limited. Some teams are just better than others. Of course it's a good idea for teams to challenge themselves and to be challenged to improve. However, mutually comparing teams might not be the best way to achieve this. But, if you have your heart set on comparing teams to stimulate them to grow, how can you best do this?

- **Performance growth.** The most important tip: if you're going to mutually compare teams, don't compare their current performance, compare their performance growth! Irrespective of its current performance, the team with the largest performance growth rate will overtake everyone when given enough time. The improvement rate is a far better way to compare teams than the current working speed.

- **Return on investment.** Compare teams based on relative values. An example is the return on investment of the team. Calculate this by dividing the profit by the costs.

- **Predictability index.** You can also apply a predictability index. Do this by dividing the forecast of a team at the start of a Sprint by the number of realized story points at the end. This indicates the reliability of a team in keeping its commitments.

- **Focus factor.** You can also calculate the focus factor. Do this by dividing the total delivered story points by the total number of worked story points. What portion of the work actually ended up in the current product? For this, you should aim at reaching at least 80%. This factor indicates how well the team focuses on the most important thing.

- **Velocity index.** Estimations between teams can't be compared because a story point in one team means something different in another team. Therefore, it's also not possible to compare the velocity (the number of completed story points per Sprint) between teams. You can make these numbers comparable by constructing an inter-team index for this.

- **Standardize the story point scale.** Sometimes it's convenient to standardize the story-point scale between teams, for example, when multiple teams work on a single product with the same Product Backlog.

- **Quality.** Sometimes it's possible to pinpoint customer satisfaction (happiness) to specific teams, but also simple quality indicators such as the number of bugs or incidents after a release can help in indicating which teams have their business in order.

- **Other examples.** Velocity growth (velocity/velocity in the first Sprint), improvement rate on value (value output/value output in the first Sprint), or potentially function points per team per Sprint.

But be careful! The performance of each team will always be different than the performance of other teams simply because some teams are faster than others. Moreover, the environment of the teams often has a bigger influence on performance than the team itself has. Comparing is only fair when the context is completely the same, and this is extremely difficult to achieve. The desire to mutually compare teams is a natural one, but usually isn't necessary if you know the differences. In the end it's not about how good they are. It's about what they do to get better.

What should you do?

- Commit to delivering the maximum value on predetermined times.
- Commit to and guard constant quality.
- Commit to and guard transparency and honesty.
- Switch from estimating and tracking progress in hours to "story points" as soon as possible.
- Advance the most important things to the front of the queue.
- Emphasize working harder doesn't improve performance while working smarter does.
- Celebrate achievements and give compliments. Put successful teams in the spotlight.
- Position yourself in a supporting and coaching role.
- Only mutually compare teams to stimulate them to improve.
- Accept that some Scrum teams will always be faster than others.
- Guide teams towards growth and improving as a team.

HOW DO YOU ENSURE QUALITY WITH SCRUM?

ASSURE QUALITY AND DOCUMENTATION THROUGH WORKING RESULTS AND A DEFINITION-OF-DONE

— CHAPTER 12 —

HOW DO YOU ENSURE QUALITY WITH SCRUM?

The responsibility for delivering quality lies with the entire Scrum team. The quality is assured by delivering a finished and working end result, every Sprint. This means a high-quality result and not some semi-finished product whose quality we try to improve later. No, the end result of every Sprint must be of high quality.

But what's quality anyway? To help decide this, Scrum defines the "Definition-of-Done". The Definition-of-Done is a list of criteria that the result needs to satisfy to be considered "done". So, this list contains things such as what documentation should be completed, which tests should have been written, and what other tests or assessments need to be completed successfully to guarantee the product is up to par.

By working in short Sprints, demonstrating that the quality is good is done more often than normal. This already has a positive effect on the quality. It helps to make sure that the product is developed with quality in mind from the start, instead of finding out the quality is not high enough later and having to mend this. Often the quality tests are mostly automated, which causes the quality to be transparent continuously.

In the end, it's about the Scrum Team being responsible for delivering quality and therefore also for making it transparent. If there's no quality, there's no value.

"Hey, do you have a minute?"

"Sure, what's up?"

"Well, I just came from one of our large customers and because of Scrum, we have issues with the quality of the product!"

"Hmmm... I doubt that. Can you explain?"

"Ever since we started working with Scrum, we can do releases more often, right?"

"Yes. What's your point?"

"Well, we used to do a big and extended test project before every release. In that project we would turn our product inside out looking for problems. We no longer do that, right?"

"No, you don't. Because we do smaller and more limited changes now between two releases we can target our testing much better. Therefore, complete system tests are no longer necessary to guarantee quality."

"That's what I thought. That's why we have a problem with the quality now. We often encounter problems with the links to other systems. When we were releasing once a year, we could involve those in charge of those systems, but they don't have time to do that every two weeks."

"Aha, so they don't check it either?"

"No, they don't have time for that. They used to do this, but it was only once or twice a year. Now we're releasing every two weeks they just put the new code live without testing anything."

"But that's a good sign! They used to test our products very thoroughly and discovered many issues. Now they don't test it anymore and just release the product without testing anything. There's no way they would do that if they didn't trust the product. I think the quality has increased. I suggest you ask them."

"I will, but how can we solve the issues we have with linking to other systems?"

"Okay, that's pretty simple. We're continuously running integration tests, system tests, and chain tests. Apparently we test the links to other systems insufficiently. I'll make some calls to find out who can give us some better insight in this. I assume they run a few automated tests themselves. Maybe we can continuously update these for them. We'll work this out. In the end we all have the same incentive: high quality."

"Okay, will you make this happen?"

"Yep. I'll call them right now!"

Working in one team prevents quality issues

Handing over work causes quality issues. One person is paid to make something while another is paid to find mistakes in it. If you optimize this process, the first person will start to work faster and sloppier and the second will find more mistakes. Every link in the chain seems to improve, but the performance of the whole chain is lower. In a chain of work, the links pass the problems from one to the other and, in the end, one of the links is blamed. But to the customer nothing has changed. He isn't any happier.

Why do we discuss this in a chapter about quality? Well, Scrum uses a vastly different approach. How? By working with cross-functional teams. The skill of every link in the chain is represented in the team. Therefore, work is no longer handed over but performed jointly by the entire team, so going from idea to implementation, from concept to cash, within a single team. This also means that teams solve their own problems. You can no longer pass the problem to someone else. You need to resolve it yourself, just like you would solve a problem in a soccer team. If one player can't keep up with the player from the opposing team, one of his teammates will have to fix that for him. Defending as an attacking player, positioning yourself more central as a fullback, and forward defending as a midfielder are examples of this. In the end, you win or lose a match as a team.

In short, the most important step in quality assurance lies with the cross-functional teams. This concept is also known as *"Drink your own champagne!"*. The team use their own product as early as possible to understand what it is like to use it, understanding the needs of the customer. The more direct the connection between the Scrum teams and the customer, the more things they have to take care of themselves. For this, Scrum uses the Definition-of-Done.

How to decide whether the quality is good?

To help ensure a quality standard, Scrum uses the Definition-of-Done (DoD), the checklist that describes the finished state. This list describes what it means when a Scrum team says something is "done" and ready to be released to the customer. It needs to be completely clear what done means. Therefore, all quality requirements and tests need to be on the checklist. What tests need to be executed successfully? What process documentation is mandatory and therefore delivered? Who has approved it? These are examples of requirements that should be on the checklist. So there can't be any doubt about the quality. If something is done, then it's finished and meets the criteria as defined in the Definition-of-Done. You're certain what it means when a team says something's finished. Who checks whether something fulfills the criteria on the checklist? That easy: the Scrum team itself. In the end, they'll be confronted with the consequences if the results aren't good enough.

Who makes the checklist? A common fallacy is that the Definition-of-Done is made by the Product Owner. However, that would make it like a traditional process: the customer defines requirements and the team makes it. In Scrum, things are different. The Development Team decides what it means for something to be done. They take responsibility for choosing high quality criteria. Subsequently they'll discuss this proposal with the Product Owner and a number of stakeholders (sometimes customers) to decide whether this Definition-of-Done is good enough. They'll also discuss what competences are missing in the team for it to be able to meet the quality criteria. It is in nobody's interest to end up with a list of criteria a team can't or won't stick to.

So all required quality criteria are on the checklist. If you don't fulfill these criteria, you can't claim something's finished. Working and tested results at the end of every Sprint is what it's all about. Therefore, the checklist is indispensable for managing quality. Make the checklist transparent and put it on the wall.

In practice, the functional quality is often put under pressure. "Does it do what it needs to do?" is then considered more important than the real quality. This will, however, end up hurting you in the long run. Taking short cuts on the quality checklist creates something known as technical debt, problems that have to be addressed at a later date. The most important countermeasure of the team is to only start working on the next item on the Product Backlog when all the current items are done and conform to the DoD. By doing so, you avoid too many things being worked on at once, which can jeopardize the quality on all fronts.

Should you automate all quality tests?

No, you don't need to automate all tests, but it is practical to automate as many as possible. In the end, you need to prove the quality is high enough. So you need to deliver high quality continuously, not just at the end. Therefore, it's worth the effort to automate this. Further, after you've gone through the effort to automate the quality tests, why not run them every day, or even more frequently? Many Scrum teams run these tests continuously. Every time anything is changed, all tests are run automatically. If you work like this and something goes wrong, you immediately know what caused it. This is an example of advancing the feedback in everything you do.

Is this always possible? Yes, of course it is, as long as you want it enough. In some cases, it can be very difficult. In some industries, it is customary to do a last certifying test before the product is released on to the market. How do you deal with this with Scrum? There is no general applicable answer for this question. However, it's always possible to find something better than not testing at all during the Sprints. Partial feedback always beats having no feedback. How do you eat an elephant? Exactly, one bite at a time.

Let's look at an example. Wikispeed builds cars using Scrum. Wikispeed's cars get the highest, five-star ratings for collision safety. And they do everything with Scrum. How do they do this? Doing a collision test every Sprint costs too much. So they do virtual collision tests based on models. And you know what's so special about this? The US government now recognizes these virtual collision simulations. Wikispeed's five-star rating is based on these virtual collision simulations. The only thing they still do outside of this is do a real physical collision test twice a year to calibrate their virtual models. Consequently, they can do collision simulations based on virtual models and use the physical collision tests to show their models are accurate. They really changed the rules of the game.

In short, it's about proving the quality of your results as often as possible. Because you aim to do it so often, it pays to automate it as much as possible. And when this is difficult: think of a way around the current rules. It's always possible to come up with a way to advance getting feedback (or the most important part of it).

Sometimes you can go so far as to completely change the rules of the game.

Bad quality costs time and money and causes even more bad quality

An important reason for the success of Scrum is that it prescribes intensively working towards working and tested results. No time is lost and wasted on the consequences of bad quality, which is revealed as bugs. It's not an effective use of you time to work on things like solving problems and looking for causes. Continuously and automatically monitoring quality pays.

Therefore, it's important to use a Definition-of-Done with clear quality requirements. It's also important that the Product Owner understand the need for this. Low quality slows teams down and is, therefore, a waste of time and money.

Because of this, teams need the time to do their work right and really finish things. This is why they are the ones who select what work from the Product Backlog to do in each Sprint. They are the ones who decide what is attainable and what's not. This is not the role of the Product Owner. The Product Owner decides what's the most important and what has the highest priority, but what is attainable in a specific Sprint is decided solely by the team. In Scrum, there's a term for cutting corners: technical debt. This is the quality debt you build by not properly finishing things. When the team slows down because of this, you're paying the interest on the technical debt.

It pays to actively monitor technical debt and work towards preventing and reducing it in every Sprint. It is advisable to express this in the effect on the teams' speed dealing with low quality. This allows the Product Owner to include it in his ordering of the Product Backlog. The "axe" of the team needs to be sharpened by clearing away the quality issues one step at a time.

What about Scrum and documentation?

The last preconception about Scrum is that nothing is documented. This is fundamentally wrong. It's just that documentation is looked at differently. Firstly, the only documentation that is created provides value immediately. So documentation that will really be used, or that is necessary for compliance reasons, is generated. Usually, this is the documentation that describes what you have made. All descriptive documentation made by the Scrum teams is written to conform to the checklist. So actually, in every Sprint the teams expand the documentation. The documentation is worked on continuously instead of at the end.

Documentation that is required by the auditor or for certification is valuable and is, therefore, included in the checklist. It's practical to not work with a long list of documents in the checklist but instead make one big document with different sections for everything that needs to be recorded. By doing so, only one document needs to be extended and updated each time. It should be checked in advance whether this is allowed. You don't want to face a nasty surprise at the end.

When you hand over work, this creates a strong urge to document things. This is very different in Scrum. By working in short cycles, focusing directly on customer value, really finishing things, and working in a cross-functional team, this urge is mostly taken away. People discuss things and start working. The knowledge needed to do this is in everyone's head because it has been discussed. Therefore, working in stable cross-functional teams prevents the need for a large part of the documentation that's usually made – the detailed specifications.

In short, quality is assured by working with a cross-functional team with close ties to the customer. Such teams need less documentation, because everyone knows what's what. Of course, what has been made is documented and continuously kept up-to-date. You never know when you need it, so descriptive documentation is important and therefore included in the checklist.

What about Scrum and architecture?

When organizations are researching Scrum, a common question is how does Scrum deal with the architecture needed to create a working solution? This is because with Scrum, many decisions are postponed until the latest responsible moment and planning in detail is done when more information is available so that the best decision can be made. In traditional environments, important decisions about the architecture are all made upfront. Therefore, it makes sense that the combination of agile and architecture feels a bit difficult at first.

Because of the flexible and agile approach of Scrum, people claim it's not possible to adhere to an architecture. This is incorrect. The main cause of this misunderstanding is that Scrum strongly differentiates itself from "Big Design Upfront". Scrum is about using the new insights you gain. Scrum assumes that much will be learned during the project and the problems will become clearer as you proceed. This implies it's best to not choose the architecture upfront, but to let it evolve during the execution of the work, when the understanding is highest.

Saying that the architecture should be described in full detail upfront and everything must be decided is nonsense. It is fine to describe the overview of the architecture and to specify a set of architectural principles that will be used in future iterations. This does mean that architecture plays a different role in Scrum, and it's still very valuable. The architect's role is also far from over. There's still a need to have someone with insight, overview, design skills, and the communication skills to help and inspire the team to make wise choices. That person needs to be an Agile architect, an architect who supports the team and actively helps the team to discover the needed architecture.

What should you always remember?

- Handing over work between teams and roles causes quality issues.
- Concept to cash, within one team, leads to quality more easily.
- Handing over work between team members is also a cause for quality issues.
- Working together on things makes achieving a level of quality easier.
- The checklist of the Scrum Team (Definition-of-Done) is an important tool for assuring high quality.
- It pays to automate the (most important) tests to make the quality continuously transparent.
- Taking away bad quality (technical debt) increases speed and saves money.
- Bad quality results in even worse quality.
- Documentation is also important with Scrum as certain documentation is valuable.
- Find out upfront how to iteratively develop documentation while still complying with mandatory standards.
- It's better to let the architecture evolve than to choose it in advance.
- Allowing the architecture to evolve is best done with guidance of an Agile architect.

HOW DOES SCRUM SCALE?

LARGE-SCALE SCRUM WITH MANY SCRUM TEAMS SHOULD BE MANAGED BY PRODUCT OWNERS, A CHIEF PRODUCT OWNER, AND A CORPORATE PRODUCT BACKLOG

— CHAPTER 13 —

HOW DOES SCRUM SCALE?

We often encounter the prejudice that Scrum doesn't scale. This would imply that while Scrum works for one or a few teams, it's hard to organize when it gets much bigger than that.

The opposite is true. Large and successful companies such as Microsoft, Google, and Philips are able to scale up to hundreds of Scrum teams. Scaling up with teams is as easy (or as hard) as any other way of scaling. It's true you need to organize a few things. Product Owners need to mutually make their backlogs fit each other. Often a Chief Product Owner is needed to make the primary choices in this. It's also desirable to construct a Corporate Backlog. Finally, managing dependencies between teams and encouraging communication between teams using a technique called Scrums of Scrums is usually also necessary. Scaling requires more coordination. However, this has nothing to do with Scrum. That's just a property of scaling.

Scrum's also useful for settings with an offshore site or other forms of distributed work. This is because it puts the focus on value and concrete results. That's very practical when you can't see each other every day or when meeting up is difficult. The same is true when you outsource everything: try to advance the most important things to the front of the queue. Steer your supplier towards producing working and valuable results quickly.

In short, Scrum not being able to scale is a myth. However, how to properly scale is something that needs to be explained well.

"Listen up. We have ten Scrum teams now and I no longer feel like I have an overview of what's going on. Who does what and is everything going okay? How is Scrum supposed to scale?"

"Overall, nothing really changes. Whether you have one team or twenty, they will all produce a working result each Sprint. This is what they do, so that's where the focus should be. The result is no longer the result of a single team, but the sum of all their results. Are you following me?"

"I think so. So all six teams of our payment product are only working on one product?"

"Yes. So the results of the six teams are just part of a single result. That single result is what you should monitor. Let the teams work out how they manage that. There is something new, though. Do you know what the extra thing is the four Product Owners now do?"

"Yes, coincidentally I know that. They coordinate. They do that every other week. They've been doing that for two months and it works pretty well. Sometimes when they're stuck, they ask my help."

"Ah, I didn't know that. Good! That's exactly how it should go. There are four of them, but they share the responsibility for the product. Sometimes that works, but often they need a Chief Product Owner. Apparently, that's you. By choosing you, they gave you something special. They gave you a steering wheel and you can now steer the product through them."

"Oh, I didn't experience it like that."

"Okay, then I know why. You don't go to the Sprint Reviews and you don't look at the backlogs they do agree on."

"That's right. I can't be there for all those meetings. That takes way too much time."

"I understand, but by doing so, you're giving up the steering wheel. Do you want to? If I were you, I'd try to get the teams to do a joint review in which they show all the highlights. If they do, you can also invite clients to this review. Also ask the Product Owners to discuss their entire backlog with you once a month. All this will cost you less than four hours a month."

"Okay, so this is how Scrum scales?"

"Exactly. Through a team of Product Owners, with a Chief Product owner, a collection of Scrum teams, and coordination between these teams, usually by the Scrum Masters."

"How can we continue to scale further?"

"In the same way. When more Chief Product Owners are needed, you need someone to manage the Chief Product Owners. It's also practical to make a backlog for the entire company and to hang that on a wall. You can also use that for doing workshops with customers and prospects. Nice and transparent!"

"I hadn't thought of that. I'm definitely going to do that. I can hang four backlogs on the wall for all four products. I'm starting to get how this works!"

"Exactly, and then you can focus on what's truly important: making sure we're all getting better together! Then they'll start hitting your targets! But we'll talk about that later."

"Yes, I'm keeping you to that. Then I also want to hear how we can use this for our teams in India..."

How to scale with many teams

When talking about scaling, there are two things to look at: size and turnaround time. On the one hand, you have to think about managing the collaboration of tens or hundreds of Scrum teams. On the other hand, you have to make sure that scaling doesn't slow the process down. Before you know it, you can end up with teams passing work to each other and taking months again for ideas to be transformed into real customer value.

When you scale Scrum and start working with many teams, you need to understand that when the focus of these teams lies only on one link in the chain, you're only optimizing one link in the entire process. So, next to organizing the collaboration of many Scrum teams, it's also important to steer these teams in an agile fashion (corporate backlogs, portfolio management, program budgeting, etc.). If you don't do this, you will only make one step in the process faster while improving the entire chain in a very limited fashion. This is also true for all steps in the process after the Scrum teams. So also things such as management and the promotion model to production should be looked at in order to fully reap the benefits of Scrum.

Having said this, how do you scale many teams? Well, the overall principle isn't very different from the case with a limited number of teams. Teams continue to be cross-functional and continue to deliver a working and tested product every Sprint. Teams still work on a single Product Backlog, which is prioritized by the Product Owner. The backlog is still estimated by the team and refining is still done in collaboration with the stakeholders, Product Owner, and end users. As far as those things are concerned, nothing changes.

There is something new, however: Product Owners will need to coordinate across teams and the teams themselves will need to coordinate to manage mutual dependencies. The aim is to try to manage things in such a way that interdependencies between teams are minimal, but there will usually be dependencies. The coordination between teams takes place in a meeting called the

"Scrum of Scrums". This is a 15-minute meeting where someone from each development team joins to coordinate the work being done across teams.

Another thing we frequently encounter is that the Scrum Masters unite and resolve backlog impediments together. This is an excellent way to realize improvements across teams. Next to this, it has an important side effect: by "drinking your own champagne", you demonstrate the agile mindset to the rest of the organization.

How to manage dependencies between teams

Scrum teams usually do this with a Scrum of Scrums in which the teams coordinate during the Sprint and keep an eye on interdependencies. We usually encounter an additional daily Scrum of Scrums, a 15-minute stand-up meeting with someone from each team. Whoever has the highest interest out of each team to join this daily Scrum of Scrums is the most appropriate person to participate. Additionally, it's common for teams to agree on a minimal Definition-of-Done across teams. The checklist is still specific to each team, but is at least as strict as this minimal Definition-of-Done. By doing so, it's clear what the minimum quality restrictions are of what is delivered by all teams, and that the result at the end of the sprint is fully integrated and working.

Much more important is the coordination at the start of the chain. Product Owners need to coordinate with each other next to ordering "their own" backlog. Coordination across backlogs is now also essential. The more deliberations and backlogs will result in more steps between idea and delivery, so the longer it takes for customer value to materialize. Therefore, try to limit the number of steps. It's best to work with a single large Product Backlog from which all teams take their work.

The Product Owners mutually coordinate their work. It can be helpful to appoint a single Chief Product Owner who is responsible for the overall backlog. Choosing one of the directors for this is practical.

Some organizations initially focus their teams on one system or set of systems. Unfortunately, real changes and new propositions usually transcend these systems. To be successful then, teams need to be able to take action across all systems. In situations where Scrum teams are restricted from taking action across all systems, we frequently encounter the reintroduction of the role of project manager. The project manager is then responsible for the overall coordination across Scrum teams and his or her primary activity is making sure all Product Owners order the right things at the right times.

It's true that officially Scrum doesn't define a project manager role. However, practice isn't a theoretical laboratory. In the end, you are the one who decides how to manage things and that's fine, as long as you realize why you make choices and try to get closer and closer to the ideal situation. In the end, the Scrum teams are able to coordinate and manage everything themselves.

How to guarantee knowledge sharing between teams

Besides making sure the work flows to the Scrum teams in the right way, allowing them to make a working product together, knowledge sharing is essential. For a limited number of teams working on a single floor, knowledge sharing usually occurs naturally. However, when the number of teams grows significantly, this won't be sufficient anymore. This is because Scrum teams have a strong inward focus and, therefore, have the tendency to look for improvements within the team. At the same time, problems that are encountered in one team are often already solved in another team. Additionally, the teams often only give limited attention to improving in specific roles or specialist competences.

To face this challenge, many organizations introduce the guild principle. Guilds are groups of likeminded people to learn and improve together. You can compare this to a goalkeeper training in soccer. Of course it's very important to improve as a team; however, to really improve as a goalkeeper, you need specialist training by a goalkeeper trainer. This is exactly how the guilds work. Guild meetings are held regularly, with once or twice a month being common. Guilds collaborate to learn and improve one theme at a time. The testing guild, for instance, will focus on themes such as: test driven development practices, tooling, automatic regression tests, etc. The goal of each guild is to improve.

For guilds, support by management is essential as well. Guild participation is the "sharpening of the axe". What if you're judged based on chopping trees 100% of the time? Will you sharpen your axe at home in the evening hours? Or is sharpening your axe part of your job? What's a good distribution between carrying out work and getting better in doing your job?

Documenting knowledge continues to be a challenge. Most people don't like to do this. However, there are some easy tricks that are often overlooked. Making a YouTube movie with a bunch of people is a fun and excellent way to document knowledge. The same goes for making a large comic. The more fun people have in guilds, the easier it will be to document the results.

How to do Scrum if you're not together?

Scrum is more difficult when working offshore or generally distanced from each other. If you can't see each other, it's more difficult to communicate, coordinate, and manage things. This is especially true when non-physical products are concerned because then it's also difficult to see where you left off. Additionally, it's much tougher to make it clear what you need or mean exactly.

However, this is exactly why Scrum is helpful for distributed work. This is because it's much more difficult to see how things are going when you're not physically together. There's only one good solution for this: finishing things. Working results are the only useful indicator of progress. So it helps tremendously to work in short Sprints. By doing so, it becomes clear far more quickly when there's a misunderstanding and it's much easier to see how things are going. This doesn't make things easier, but it does make everything transparent.

Additionally, you need the right technical equipment. There is a lot of good equipment available that helps to greatly reduce the perception of distance. Examples are a continuous open video connection (virtual window) and good quality video conferencing tooling. Don't cut corners on these things. Making mistakes in your product will cost much more than these communication tools cost.

The same holds for traveling. Flying somewhere costs money, but this is easily earned back by the time you save by being able to meet up face-to-face. Therefore, it's advisable when working with Scrum in offshore settings to allow the teams to make traveling decisions. Everyone should be allowed to travel to a colleague when necessary. Avoid difficult procedures with required permissions and autographs. Remember, *"Individuals and interactions over processes and tools..."*

An important tip: When working with Scrum in multiple locations, put the distance inside the team boundary. With this, we mean you should avoid creating a Scrum team in one location and a Scrum team in the other, because this will prevent those teams from running into each other. This makes coordinating difficult and when problems occur, the teams will often point fingers at each other. Therefore, build Scrum teams with team members in both locations. This will guarantee that members from all teams will be present in both locations. Also make sure that all teams have team members within walking distance from the end users or client. This way each team will be able to quickly ask for clarification.

A final thing: Don't alter the Scrum meetings because of the distributed collaboration. The meetings are essential for Scrum to work. When it's difficult to do so, still don't adapt the meetings. When the teams are in very different time zones, share the pain of the unfavorable time of the day between both locations. If having a Daily Scrum is difficult, find out why it's difficult and fix this. Don't decrease the frequency of the Daily Scrum; it's called the Daily Scrum for a reason. Altering meetings leads to Scrum not being effective. Always avoid this!

How to do Scrum when nearly everything is outsourced?

Many organizations no longer do the work themselves. They outsource everything. If you want to work with Scrum in such a situation, you'll need to impose Scrum on the supplier. This is probably not a good idea. Before you know it, Scrum is the goal instead of a means to an end.

It's beyond the scope of this book to work out all aspects of agile commissioning. What you can do is make clear that you aim to steer based on the agile principles and the most important properties of Scrum:

- At least every month, the supplier needs to deliver a working and tested product.
- The supplier first finishes the most valuable thing.
- Working together with the supplier, the upcoming work is made sufficiently small and detailed for the supplier to be able to work on and finish multiple things a week.
- Working results are shown to the supplier and to stakeholders.
- Don't specify the end result in great detail in advance.
- Make collaboration central in the relationship with the supplier.
- Appoint someone to make choices and decide on priorities for the supplier.
- Try to actively learn in collaboration with the supplier and actively apply the learned lessons in short cycles.
- Coordinate daily to make sure what's being worked on is feasible and check whether someone needs help.
- Help the supplier by updating the priorities and with additional choices when the plan is no longer feasible.
- Try to minimize the number of changes in personnel and keep the teams as stable as possible.
- Make contractual agreements with respect to team composition, required competences in the teams, and changes in team composition by the supplier.

What should you do?

- Manage coordination across Product Owners when scaling Scrum to many teams.
- Appoint a director as Chief Product Owner.
- Construct Product Backlogs tied to one global Corporate Backlog.
- Help Scrum Masters to improve led by one Super Scrum Master.
- Try to minimize dependencies during Sprints as much as possible.
- Facilitate a Scrum of Scrums to help teams to coordinate during Sprints.
- Facilitate guilds to allow specialist competence improvement to take place.
- Don't alter Scrum because the work is done in more than one physical location.
- Try to put the distance inside the teams instead of between the teams.
- Make the teams responsible for traveling decisions; remove administrative impediments.
- Study agile commissioning when you outsource most of your work.
- Don't force Scrum on the supplier, but instead ask the supplier to work in short iterations with working results.

HOW TO CONVINCE OTHERS OF THE VALUE OF SCRUM?

ALLOW EVERYONE TO EXPERIENCE SCRUM FOR THEMSELVES: FINISHING THE MOST VALUABLE THING COMPLETELY WITH A TEAM!

— CHAPTER 14 —

HOW TO CONVINCE OTHERS OF THE VALUE OF SCRUM?

It isn't always easy to convince others of the value of Scrum. You're not the first one who comes along to propose a new approach that will "really" solve all problems. The past has shown this usually isn't the case. Most clients have experience with suppliers that use a method as an excuse. "The operation's a success but the patient has died." "The project may have failed but we executed the method to the letter, so pay up!"

When you explain Scrum to clients, they think they heard it all before. They know the end result: they'll be unhappy and the supplier will act all innocent. So don't do it.

But then how should you convince others? That's easy: let them experience it works! Even within tight boundaries, it's possible to work with Scrum in some form. Focus on working on the most valuable thing first and really finishing this, followed by a demonstration. When you've done this, you can continue and then it will become useful to explain what you're doing.

Letting go of a plan-driven way of thinking is a very special change. It's not strange people are skeptical about this change and ask critical questions. At the same time, resistance means energy, so that's a good sign. Those who initially resist Scrum the most regularly end up being the most important ambassadors when they've experienced the power of Scrum.

"Scrum may be useful to development teams but outside of development, its value is really limited. For example, for sales it's completely useless."

"You shouldn't consider a sales team a Scrum team. A sales team isn't cross-functional. More is needed to make a client happy than just sales. Sales is a function. One step in the process."

"So?"

"So you should explore whether we can create teams that are truly cross-functional. Why don't you try Scrum out for a month in your management team? Your team consists of many different disciplines. How often do you talk to each other?"

"Well, officially once a week, but that's only an hour so just enough to discuss the most prominent problems. Therefore, the meeting often runs late. Fortunately, we have a two-day meeting every three months. That's usually the only time we have time to really coordinate."

"Exactly, so you're trying to coordinate once a week, but you can't and therefore do it once every three months. You should try moving in the opposite direction. Don't meet up less but more frequently. You could try meeting every day."

"No we can't!! I'm not going to have a meeting of more than an hour every day!"

"No, not an hour. Fifteen minutes. Just do a stand-up meeting with the management team. Why wouldn't that work for you? Or don't you need each other's help?"

Of course we do. Often the challenges we face are cross-disciplinary. This makes sense because otherwise you would just solve it yourself. So coordinating daily? Can we do that by phone?"

"If that's the only way. Have a phone call with the management team between 8.30 and 8.45 every day and those that are in the office physically stand together as you should with a stand-up meeting. Is that a good idea?"

"Hmmm... it's worth a try. And it brings another benefit."

"It does?"

"Well, I've noticed half the management team doesn't really get Scrum and doesn't seem to want to get it. I think this is because they don't experience it. If we do this, they will. I like to give it a try."

"Shall I guide the first week?"

"Good idea, it will probably be a bit strange in the beginning. By the way, Monday is the management meeting. Could you start facilitating our meetings then? We've already discussed introducing an external chairman. We hope this will help us to keep the meeting within the scheduled time."

"Okay, fine. And you know what? We won't mention Scrum at all. That will just scare people off. We'll make a plan with post-its and agree to call each other for 15 minutes for the first week. Just to try it out. Then we'll go from there. If everyone likes it, we'll explain Scrum then. Good idea?"

"Excellent idea. See you Monday nine o'clock in the boardroom!"

How to explain Scrum to customers and stakeholders?

Don't do this until later! Don't try to explain Scrum to customers unless they specifically ask for this. Trying to explain it will just make you look like the next bureaucrat who's trying to hide behind a process. Customers don't want excuses. Customers want valuable results of good quality, with the highest value for the lowest price. That's it. Customers don't want Scrum.

So what should you do? We advise not to change much from how you've been interacting with customers in the past. Make an offer, estimates, etc., etc. If customers haven't heard of Scrum, don't confuse them. Just document what they think they need and negotiate a price. However, you should ask two things:

> **First:** Who can help us decide what we deliver *sooner*? Indicate you're able to deliver working results sooner and, therefore, would like to do the most valuable thing first. They'll need to provide input for this. You can propose to do an introductory workshop for this followed by two one-hour meetings with two weeks between these meetings.

> **Second:** How can we show you during the project what we already completed to check whether we are on schedule? Emphasize end users need to be involved to give you feedback and potentially include these new insights into the final product.

When convincing the customer of these two small changes you can use terms such as steering, advancing, quality control, showing progress, demonstrating results, etc. Try to give your customer more control and make course changes possible. Subsequently, you'll demonstrate a working and tested result every two weeks. Moreover, you give the customer the option to finish the most important things sooner. By doing so, you get feedback earlier and enable the customer to steer based on value.

This will automatically cause the customer to try to take control (usually after three Sprints). Your customer will opportunistically try to use your Sprints for his own benefit.

Pay attention: This is the moment you've been waiting for! This is moments you'll make new agreements. This is the moment you'll finally explain Scrum and make agreements on how to collaborate better. This is the moment to focus on the left side of the *Agile Manifesto*. From *"contract negotiation"* and *"following a plan"* to *"customer collaboration"* and *"responding to change"*! Be very aware of this. We started by telling you to not explain Scrum but this is the time to do so.

Moreover, this is the moment in which you cannot afford to forget to explain Scrum!

Eight measures to let stakeholders experience Scrum

It's impossible to convince others; they'll need to convince themselves. What you can do is spark their curiosity. A number of concrete measures you can take to help others to convince themselves are:

1. **Workshop.** A convenient measure is to organize an Agile Awareness or Scrum workshop. You could make the workshop broader and make it about value improvement or organization flexibility. Decide for yourself what's most appropriate. You're "selling" Scrum, so try to pinpoint the workshop on the biggest pain point experienced in the organization. People will only change their behavior to avoid pain or to increase pleasure.

2. **Excursion.** Try to go on an excursion. The excursion can be to another organization or another department that already works with Scrum. Visiting another organization, getting a taste of their enthusiasm, and perceiving the transparency will do wonders. There's only so much you can achieve by

enthusiastically talking about Scrum. Visiting a real team in a real environment is much more effective.

3. **Movie.** Show a movie. Don't send the link, because no one will watch the movie if you do. Invite people to a lunch or show the movie at the yearly company gathering. YouTube is full of movies about Scrum, from team Wikispeed, which builds cars, to a Scrum Master head-butting everyone, to training videos in the form of a presentation, to other ways to visualize the power of Scrum.

4. **Book.** You can also hand out a small book to everyone. This book is the best choice of course (...) but Scrum, a travel companion, The power of Scrum, Scrum for Dummies, Scrum Essentials, and Working Software in 30 days are also good choices.

5. **Game/simulation.** As part of the theme, "experience it first" playing a Scrum game can be nice. A commonly used game is the Marshmallow Challenge to teach people why iterations aren't natural to most people.

6. **Asking questions.** Applying this measure requires some experience, but can be very effective. The trick is to ask questions about what happens when you don't change anything. In a way, you're trying to amplify the pain that's felt. Examples of good questions are: What if we get a project twice the size of what we're doing now? Why can't we deal with changes in a fast and easy fashion? Why do changes slow down our projects? How can we get to production in half the time?

7. **Pilot.** Trying it out can be helpful. Label it pilot, proof of concept, experiment, or something. What you're doing is

creating a relatively risk-free environment to experience Scrum first hand and see what it can achieve. Pilots have one big disadvantage: they don't matter. If a pilot is successful, people can always say it wasn't representative.

8. **Just do it.** This is usually the best solution. Take a project, product, or department that is doing terrible as it is. In such an environment, you can really show how it works by making a difference. Almost all aspects of Scrum can be immediately applied. Finishing things quickly, starting with the most valuable thing first, learning in short cycles, collaborating with the customer, stakeholders, and end users will always work. When people start asking why you are successful while others weren't is when you start explaining Scrum.

How to deal with people who refuse to participate with Scrum?

The worst thing to do in such a situation is to devise a solution to make the symptom go away. For example, allow someone who doesn't want to be in a Scrum team to be a one-man Scrum team or to make him an "internal advisor".

Most of the work we do is just too hard to do alone. Cross-functional teams are the answer to that. That's not open to discussion. So not being part of a team is not an option. Outside of this, everyone is allowed to contribute towards team makeup but everyone is part of a Scrum team and all Scrum teams are complete. Recognize that teams offer a transparency that's very nice but can be scary in the beginning. It's impossible to hide in a team. All the work is on the Product Backlog and this work is taken on by the entire team so it's impossible to avoid. Resistance against being part of a team is frequently a symptom of being afraid of transparency or being afraid that the transparency will be used against you.

What if someone is not a team player? What if we're dealing with a soloist expert who can't work in a team, but is very valuable on his own? These are the people of whom you're always afraid they'll leave or have a ski accident. These are the people whose knowledge is indispensable. These are also the people whose prime responsibility should be to make themselves dispensable. They are simply too important and are as such a risk for continuity of the organization. The best way to do this is by being part of a team and sharing their knowledge with others.

Be clear in explaining there's no alternative to being part of a Scrum team. Remember, not being able to work in a team or in the best interest of a team also existed before; it just wasn't visible on a daily basis. Stable Scrum teams make that problem visible so it can be dealt with. All the discussions you have with people about not wanting to be part of a Scrum team are discussions that will make the whole better. When all people are able to successfully contribute in a team, this will greatly improve the effectiveness of your organization.

Scrum fundamentally changes the division of labor. The people no longer go to the work but the work goes to the people. This will only work with stable Scrum teams. If you break this fundamental principle by allowing people to work outside of Scrum teams, you're making life very difficult for yourself. If you do so you'll still have the "resource" puzzle you've always had in addition to the new team dynamics. So just say no. Everything should be organized around Scrum teams.

Organize everything with stable cross-functional Scrum teams.

What should you do?

- Don't explain Scrum as a process guarantee to stay within your budget and planning.
- Don't explain Scrum until people start asking why you're able to deliver predictable results where others have failed.
- Don't condemn resistance: resistance indicates energy and involvement.
- Organize workshops for stakeholders to explain Scrum in relation to the existing pain points in the organization.
- Try to go on an excursion to another organization or department that works with Scrum.
- Expand the knowledge of people using a video, book, or simulation.
- Show that Scrum works. Start with Scrum in a situation with a big problem. This is where it's most likely to prove itself.
- Address it when people show anti-team behavior.
- Explicitly communicate that being a team player is a prerequisite for success.
- Don't accept individuals positioning themselves outside of teams.
- Allow everyone to experience the power of Scrum for themselves.

EPILOGUE

We are passionately involved in introducing and training agility on a daily basis. For us, Scrum is an excellent first step towards high effectiveness and agility. In the last years, we found that support and vision of management is essential in achieving this. It is necessary for management to fully comprehend Scrum and help the Scrum teams to be successful.

We are 110% convinced that agility will make the difference in the next decades. Because of the increasing power and influence of social media and the profound computerization of our society, it is difficult to survive if you are unable to quickly respond to change. In an ever-changing and increasingly small world, survival of the fittest is the norm. We hope this book helps in this.

Nobody ever writes a book alone. Inspiration comes from many people and our learning experiences have occurred in the presence of many. It is impossible to mention everyone we want to thank here. Nevertheless, there are a few people we like to thank specifically:

Simon Reindl, an excellent scrum.org trainer and Agile coach, who helped us out with a detailed review of the English version of this book.

Kevin Dullemond, who helped us out with an initial translation of the book.

Eelco Rustenburg, Astrid Claessen, and **Paul Kuijten** who, based on their experience in Agile coaching, have helped us with a detailed review of the first version of this book.

All supervisors, managers, and directors who have taken a critical look at this book and have given us indispensable suggestions for additions and improvements: **Ruud Bos, Henk Richmond, Ronald Voets, Marieke Teerds, Ronny Kennes, Svenja de Vos, Irene Tiepel,** and **Leo van der Heijden**. Additionally, we'd like to thank **Betteke van Ruler** who looked at the manuscript without the bias that comes with a background in IT. Of course, we want to thank you all for recommending quotes as well.

All CEOs and CIOs who critically read our book and were prepared to write a foreword: **Gunther Verheijen, Ken Schwaber, Ron van Kemenade, Jeroen Tas, Vikram Kapoor,** and **Simon Reindl**. We are proud of your contributions and your help!

We also want to thank all our colleagues at Prowareness who helped us in making the inexhaustible list of management questions. In the end, this list of questions has been our primary source for determining what to discuss in this book.

Vasco Duarte at Happy Melly Express and all his colleagues involved in bringing this book to the market. Thanks to **Marja Hautala** for her creative touch. **Marcel Roozeboom** for publishing this book in the Netherlands and his critical input with respect to the tone and design.

We especially want to thank our families. Without their support it would have been impossible for us to go through the effort of doing our job and the additional steps necessary for writing this book.

Finally, we want to address you. Yes you, our reader. Of course, thanks for the time and energy you have taken to work your way through our book. Thanks for being prepared to read this book and if you intend to hand the book to future readers, thanks for that as well.

We'd like to emphasize one thing to you at the end of this book: your leadership is crucial for making Scrum a success. This book is the contribution we can give you in this.

Now it is up to you!

It won't always be easy to start working with Scrum. However, try to find support in Darwin's words, which may apply more today than ever: *"It is not the strongest of species that survives, nor the most intelligent. It is the one that is the most adaptable to change."*

We wish you all the energy and decisiveness you need to create valuable results in our dynamic world, and hope this book will be both support and inspiration for you.

Delft, October 2014

Rini van Solingen
Rob van Lanen

ABOUT THE AUTHORS

Rini van Solingen (Prof. Dr.) is a part-time full professor in Global Software Engineering at the Delft University of Technology, where he heads the research and education regarding worldwide-distributed software teams. Rini is also CTO at Prowareness (www.scrum.nl), where he helps, together with his colleagues in the Netherlands, Germany, India, and the United States, to quickly deliver working and valuable results for and with customers. He also advises management teams on this subject. He is always happy to give lectures or lead training courses or workshops, so feel free to invite him.

Next to his work for Prowareness and the TU Delft, Rini actively works for the "Logeerplezier" foundation, which he founded together with his wife Patricia. Logeerplezier arranges holiday homes and sleepovers for handicapped children and their families.

Together with Eelco Rustenberg and Jeff Sutherland, Rini published The Power of Scrum in 2010. Rini blogs at www.rinivansolingen.com and can be followed on Twitter (@solingen) or via his YouTube channel.

Of course you can also send Rini an email at rini@scrum.nl or d.m.vansolingen@tudelft.nl. Feel free to approach Rini to ask a question or have a discussion. He likes hearing from you and usually responds faster than you would expect.

Rob van Lanen is an Entrepreneur and member of the leadership team at Prowareness. Additionally, he is a Professional Scrum Trainer for scrum.org. As a Management Coach, Rob enthusiastically works towards improving the organization of the Prowareness customers. Nowadays he is more frequently presenting in boardrooms because from there it is possible to realize support for organizational change. As a Change Agent, he contributes his passion and experience with Prowareness to jointly take the next step in the mission to spread agility across the world.

As a Professional Scrum Trainer (PST), Rob is certified by scrum.org to give specialist trainings for the Scrum Master (PSM) and Product Owner (PSPO) roles. To be able to do this, he was trained by Ken Schwaber, co-creator of Scrum and CEO of scrum.org, the training institute for Scrum. Rob puts a lot of passion and energy in his trainings, which is appreciated by his students.

Rob is also a husband, father, son, brother, and friend. You can learn more about him by following him on Twitter (@robvanlanen) and you can also contact him via email at rob@scrum.nl.

Printed in Poland
by Amazon Fulfillment
Poland Sp. z o.o., Wrocław